THE
TWO FRENCH
REVOLUTIONS
1789–1796

THE
TWO FRENCH
REVOLUTIONS
1789–1796

by *Guglielmo Ferrero*

EDITED BY *Luc Monnier*

TRANSLATED FROM THE FRENCH
BY *Samuel J. Hurwitz*

WITH A FOREWORD BY *Crane Brinton*

Basic Books, Inc., PUBLISHERS

NEW YORK · LONDON

Foreword

CRANE BRINTON

Guglielmo Ferrero, Italian historian and journalist, was, at the beginning of this century, very well known indeed all over what was then not yet commonly called the Western world. Had *Time* magazine existed in the days of Theodore Roosevelt, Ferrero would undoubtedly have made its cover and had his cover story. As it was, his studies of ancient Rome, and especially his big five-volume work, *The Greatness and Decline of Rome,* translated into English as soon as its publication in Italian was completed in 1907, were favorite subjects for the lurid old "Sunday supplements" of the Hearst and the Pulitzer newspapers. I still have a memory of some sort of childish confusion between what the artists for one of them, in a piece on Ferrero, had made of what Nero did to Rome and what Nature had just done to San Francisco.

For Ferrero was a determined comparative historian. He managed in these studies of Roman history to bring in Tammany Hall, Teddy Roosevelt, the British Empire, and many of the names that figure in this book on the two French Revolutions. He had early collaborated with his father-in-law, the criminologist Cesare Lombroso, whose main work sought to establish that criminals are readily recognizable by external physiological signs and who is therefore probably now irretrievably forgotten. Ferrero himself has so far been forgotten that he has almost lost what the late W. C. Abbott called, in an admirable title for his essays on some minor figures in British history, "conflicts with oblivion." He has not, however, quite lost his own conflict with oblivion or this book would not appear in English a quarter of a century after his death in 1942.

Ferrero still has something to say to this generation, as he had to his own. He did not always say it gracefully or diplomatically, though he rarely said it obscurely. In his own time he was a most controversial figure, but this fact alone would hardly explain the comparative obscurity of his later years. Indeed, the problem of what kinds of historical writing survive in these days is a difficult and interesting one. It is hard to name a historian of the last century or so who is accepted by the public as a "classic" in the sense that Gibbon, Michelet, and Macaulay are accepted as classics. No doubt the obvious and commonly given answer is part of a full answer: "scientific" academic and professional history, which makes up the great bulk of written history today and has done so for almost all of the nineteenth century, deliberately avoids appeal to the general reader, insisting on its achievement as true science. But as science it has so far come nowhere near producing one of those great culture-heroes, unread and unreadable directly by the public, but at least as much culture-heroes for that public as any artist or literary figure of the past—Darwin, Einstein, Freud, and their peers. Moreover, the professional academic historians are scornful of those who do write for the great public. For most of his professional critics, Ferrero has never been anything but a "journalist," which is, along with "essayist," the great smear word among us historians.

Still, there must be other contributory reasons for Ferrero's long eclipse. He produced relatively little in the two decades following his big book on Roman history, and when in the 1930's he wrote in exile in Geneva a series of books, in French, for which this one is a kind of introduction, he did not quite strike the right note for a generation undergoing the great depression and about to undergo a great world war. The dangers of breaking with things established were far from worrisome to a generation that had quite other worries. Ferrero's trilogy on Europe after the Reign of Terror of the great French Revolution—*Aventure* (1933), *Reconstruction* (1940), *Pouvoir* (1942)—is centered on the damage a great social upheaval does to whatever holds men together in society. The present book, as his pupil Luc Monnier explains in the preface, is based on Ferrero's own very full notes for lectures given at the University of Geneva. It is concerned with the great events that preceded and set the problems dealt with in the trilogy. The main concepts Ferrero developed in the longer work are here clearly stated. They center on a word often repeated here, "legitimacy." There was little in Ferrero's background to prepare him for understanding, let alone sympathizing with, a concept so completely identified in the nineteenth century with European conservatism. He had grown up in the atmosphere of European liberalism, which, as his country-man Guido de Ruggiero has pointed out, is not quite the same thing as British liberalism. Especially in lands formally Catholic, the European liberal was anything but tolerant of the established religion. Ferrero was anti-clerical, doctrinaire in his belief in science and progress, not averse to the use of authority against reactionaries, an opinionated partisan of the rationalistic inheritance of the Enlightenment—and of the French Revolution as a whole. Then, in his middle age, came the totalitarian revolutions—Russian, Italian, German, Spanish. Ferrero himself was from the start against Mussolini; but his hatred for fascism did not impel him toward communism. When he finally succeeded in leaving fascist Italy in 1930 and settling in Geneva, he had joined the ranks of those who, though unable to accept any of the new forms of totalitarian polity, unable to throw over in entirety their youthful faith in democracy and progress, turned to the world crisis of the late eighteenth century and after for some light on what had apparently gone wrong with both democracy and progress. Italy produced two others who join with Ferrero in their basic position: the "principles of 1776 and 1789" have simply not worked out as men hoped they would as recently as the end of the nineteenth century. Both Pareto and Mosca—neither, incidentally, as forgotten as was Ferrero—compromised themselves with fascism, though neither was the wholehearted reactionary they have often been held to be by orthodox democrats. Ferrero never compromised with fascism, no more than did another remarkable Italian exile, Gaetano Salvemini; but whereas Salvemini, who lived to return in triumph to his university, remained to the end of his life a fine ripe old-fashioned Italian liberal, ironic, anticlerical, antisocialist, and still hopeful for democracy, Ferrero came to hold that something had to be added to his political inheritance of liberalism.

In the trilogy he put his position in a characteristic figure of speech. In a normal society, order is maintained, the laws are generally observed, not from fear of authority, nor even out of respect for such authority, nor out of mere habit, nor of anything so simple as any of these, but because the myriad human interrelations in such a society, though they tie men together, hold them together like "silken threads." These are not felt as burdensome, indeed hardly felt at all. In such a society authority is "legitimate." When, however, conscious discontent arises in a society—in part at least usually because those in authority fail to adapt fast enough to changes that are creeping in and producing maladjustments—a revolution breaks out, and the network of silken threads is cut. If the revolution falls into the hands of extremists, as did the French Revolution, that network is almost wholly destroyed. But men in any society have to have something to hold them together, and therefore, legitimacy and its silken threads having been destroyed, a dictatorship forges its "iron bonds," which are indeed felt, but which also hold. Cromwell, Napoleon, Mussolini, Lenin, Stalin, were all "illegitimate," and all were forced to govern by force, fear, and fraud.

Ferrero's "Two French Revolutions" were of course that of 1789, usually called the moderate phase of the total revolution, and that which came to power in 1792 and soon turned into the Reign of Terror, the revolution of the extremists. Ferrero clearly sympathizes with the aims of the men who peacefully in May and June 1789 converted the outdated medieval consultative Estates-General, called by the hard-pressed Louis XVI, into the National or Constituent Assembly of the French nation. He does not attempt an apology for the old regime, which he holds had so far failed in its task of government as to make the work of the Constituent Assembly absolutely necessary. But he does maintain that the Constituent Assembly failed to establish what he calls legitimacy, that as the months went by and as in 1792 France got involved in a major European war, what happened was precisely the complete destruction of the web of silken threads that had kept France together. The men who led the second revolution had no chance, and in a sense no desire, and probably no competence, to re-establish the web of legitimacy. The Terror was a relatively inefficient and inhuman form of dictatorship, which shortly gave way to the more effective tyranny of a Napoleon.

Ferrero develops this thesis, which I have necessarily simplified, with interesting and often pungent detail. He is almost always readable. This book has its faults, as has all of his work, especially when judged from the point of view of the conventions of historical writing today. This is certainly not swashbuckling romantic history; there is here no trace of the Scarlet Pimpernel or of Scaramouche. But neither is it quite in the Rankean tradition of temperate, unemphatic narrative history that makes no obvious moral judgments, and that altogether eschews comparisons of one epoch with another. Ferrero was not meticulous about his footnotes, nor exacting in his choice of authorities. Even in terms of pure scholarship, however, he does not deserve the condemnation he has often had. He was a wide and omnivorous reader in this field of history, and his store of facts was a good one. He was always the moralist, at times the preacher, and he never hesitated to make what in a current cliché are called value judgments. They are good democratic value judgments. For surely a democracy has got to hold itself together with his silken threads. A totalitarian democracy, a democracy ruled by force and torn by violence, a democracy without its own legitimacy—all these are not so much contradictions in terms as intolerable strains on human emotions. They are not signs of a long life to come for any such society. That is why this book is worth reading today.

November 1967

Editor's Preface

Guglielmo Ferrero reserved a special place in his writings for the French Revolution. It was for him a cardinal event which continues to weigh heavily upon the world of today. In order to grasp its full consequences, it is necessary to have lived through World War I. At first sight the war seems to be an incoherent succession of grandiose and outrageous events resulting in the destruction, in 1917 and 1918, of the great ruling dynasties. The revolutions which followed the collapse of the European monarchical system sharply illuminated this great drama. Was not Europe in 1918 reliving the tragedy that had befallen France when it attempted to establish a republic after the fall of Louis XVI? "From 1919 onward, throughout most of Europe, as in France after 1789," wrote Ferrero in his book *Pouvoir,* "the difficulty of organizing a republic in countries steeped in the monarchical traditions gave rise to all sorts of disorders, and resulted finally in the creation of revolutionary governments. It was these revolutionary governments which finally unleashed World War II, and for the same reasons and in ways similar to those of the French Revolution."

It was these events, to which Ferrero was a witness and of which he was to be the victim, which rendered intelligible to him the drama of 1789 and enabled him to discover its profound significance. The French Revolution became the subject of his studies and meditations. In the French Revolution, he sought an explanation of the confusion of the contemporary world. Ferrero maintained that a majority of historians who have studied the Revolution lived in the years from 1815 to 1914, a period that, except for a few years, was one of peace and general security. They were thus unable to understand the psychological phenomena that accompany great political and social upheavals. They lacked the experience to understand the particular "climate" of revolutions. It was this history which Ferrero intended to rewrite before he died on August 3, 1942.

Several weeks earlier, he had asked me to undertake this work with him. Ferrero, who had other projects in mind as well, did not want to devote too much time to this one. I accepted eagerly. He sent me the notes of his courses on the French Revolution and charged me with editing them. The editing was to be done under his direction and in accordance with his instructions as the work proceeded. He reserved the right to modify the manuscript as he deemed necessary. He had already given me some indication of the general arrangement of the work, and, with the coming of vacation time, he invited me to visit him at Mont-Pèlerin, where he was spending the summer, to plan the first chapters. I kept the appointment only to find Ferrero on his deathbed.

I had to do the work alone, therefore. The task was

xiv

not without its perils. There was always the risk of betraying the thought of my teacher and misunderstanding his true intentions. Madame Ferrero dispelled my qualms and displayed a great confidence in me to which I fear I have poorly responded. Due to unforeseen circumstances there has been a long delay in completing this work. It is thanks to the support of the Faculty of Letters at Geneva that the work now appears. I thank them for the homage rendered to the memory of one who served them with such fervor and luster.

This volume is not the history of the French Revolution which Ferrero would have given us had he lived. It is only a rough sketch. It is based on the notes of the last courses Ferrero gave at the University of Geneva, in the midst of the war, during four consecutive semesters from 1940 to 1942. I have worked from typewritten summaries of his lectures—the last of which were annotated by him.

While editing these notes, I have often thought with twinges of regret about what Ferrero would have done had he been alive. Not only would he have corrected more than one error which I have allowed to pass, and made necessary deletions, and placed a particular event in its proper perspective, giving to it a significance which I was not able to give it, but he would have elaborated with all necessary nuances on ideas to which he had only briefly alluded in his notes. Above all, he would have communicated to this necessarily condensed account that *élan,* that passion, which has so greatly animated his work and which carries us along so irresistibly.

In reading these pages, the reader should remember that the courses that gave birth to them go back ten years and the thought of war is ever present. The reader will find ideas which today are familiar but which were scarcely known when Ferrero presented them in his courses and writings. If since then these ideas have become known to a large audience, this is due to events of the last ten years which have so startlingly confirmed them.

The work which I have entitled *The Two French Revolutions* will serve to complete the three previous books written by Ferrero at Geneva: *Aventure* (1936), *Reconstruction* (1940), and *Pouvoir* (1942).* Chronologically, it comes before *Aventure*, to which it serves as an introduction.

Ferrero's Geneva writings present a remarkable unity. He takes and develops the same great themes in each of his four volumes. We follow the line of thought, which probes and questions, impatient of all conventions, avidly seeking better understanding, irresistibly attracted to the mysteries of our human condition, indefatigably opening a path in the thickets of history to attain the summit and so be able to realize eternal truths.

For Ferrero, history was not a pure science which found its justification within itself. Nor was it a fascinating reconstruction of the past. It was his means of engag-

---

* Published in English translation, respectively, as: *The Gamble: Bonaparte in Italy, 1796–1797* (New York, 1939); *The Reconstruction of Europe* (New York, 1941); and *The Principles of Power* (New York, 1942).

ing in action, of serving and fighting. I say that it was also the great adventure of his life, in which he was totally engaged, as were his wife and children with him.

The study of the past was justified in his eyes to the extent that it affected our destiny. He discarded all superfluous matters, to deal with those essential problems which exist as long as humanity exists. That is why his teachings always evoked such a profound echo in his students. When he spoke of Mirabeau, Talleyrand, or Napoleon, it was our world which he was endeavoring to make us understand. Not only the cause of the people of the Revolution, but our own. Ferrero wanted to make us realize our obligations as human beings and as citizens. If he spoke of the past to explain the present, the experience of the present aided him in grasping the past. In this constant interchange between the past and the actuality of the present there is unfolded, before our astonished gaze, our entire human destiny. At times his message seems to come from a greater distance and to pass beyond us. If indeed he raises us to unknown heights, it is because as a historian he was also a great poet.

Geneva   *Luc Monnier*
January 30, 1951

Contents

PART I   *The First Revolution*   *1*

1. *The Collapse of Monarchical Legitimacy*   *3*
2. *The Constituent Assembly*   *30*
3. *The Revolution and Europe*   *66*
4. *The Convention*   *97*
5. *The Uprising of June 2, 1793*   *131*

PART II   *The Second Revolution*   *153*

1. *The Revolutionary Government*   *155*
2. *Robespierre*   *183*
3. *The Thermidorian Reaction*   *203*

INDEX   *229*

PART I

The First Revolution

CHAPTER 1
The Collapse
of Monarchical Legitimacy

The history of the nineteenth and twentieth centuries
stems directly or indirectly from the French Revolution,
defined as the aggregate of the extraordinary events that
convulsed Europe from 1789 until the close of the Congress of Vienna in 1815. It is impossible to understand this
history without first understanding the French Revolution. But how to understand it? Where to find the gauge
that would enable us to compare the various accounts of
events, to evaluate their importance, to judge the good or
evil to which they gave rise? Until now the French Revolution has been considered from the standpoint of the
great political interests which it fostered or fought, or the

favorable or adverse passions which it aroused for a century. All the histories of the French Revolution were written in this spirit, and the right to such a point of view cannot be argued. But today we realize that it does not help us to understand the true import of events. The histories of the Revolution are divided into two categories: those of the Right and those of the Left. The two versions, from which the intellectual elite have taken their principal arguments for or against, became fixed during the nineteenth century.

The version of the Right is essentially critical. It regards the Revolution as a gigantic aberration, as a fit of folly to which France fell victim at the end of the eighteenth century. In general, it looks with favor upon the Old Regime, which it regards almost as an unrecognized paradise. The version of the Left, on the other hand, looks upon the Revolution as a magnificent effort to liberate mankind from the bonds of servitude that until then constrained it.

If one accepts the point of view of the historians of the Right that the Revolution was an act of folly, it still remains for them to explain why it was able to produce such great turmoil. The French are neither more foolish nor more wise than other peoples, and they have no taste for anarchy. The historians of the Right attribute the Revolution to the philosophy of the eighteenth century as popularized in the works of Voltaire, Diderot, and Rousseau. Taine finds Rousseau's *Social Contract,* in particular, to be responsible. It is undeniable that this literature exer-

4

cised a profound influence on the intellectual elite that led or seemed to direct the Revolution. But the masses read neither the *Social Contract* nor the other revolutionary works of the eighteenth century. And it cannot be denied that the French Revolution was a great mass movement. The weakness of the version of the Right is that it does not provide an explanation for the collapse of the oldest civilization in Europe.

As for the version of the Left, it also is too simple. It assumes the enslavement of man from the beginning of history until 1789. Was humanity really condemned until then to suffer as slaves from tyrannical, arbitrary, and cruel forces? This remains to be proven. One hundred and fifty years later, are we not moving toward a new slavery?

The Revolution certainly brought significant changes in Europe. The two most important were the replacement of the hereditary principle by the elective principle in the conferment of power and the introduction of what today we call the right of opposition. Can it be said that without the elective principle and the right of opposition the subjects of the Old Regime were miserable slaves? Society then was neither unhappier nor happier than it is at present. An authoritarian regime is not necessarily tyrannical, oppressive, or arbitrary. Under the Old Regime there were other guarantees against the abuse of power. Besides, it was a much weaker government than exists today. And we must not forget that a most wonderful civilization flourished then.

Evidently both explanations, that of the Right and that of the Left, are insufficient. One must look further. But how? One can only understand a great event by its eventual consequences, and these often are not evident until long afterward. At the end of World War I an old Chinese mandarin in Peking listened, silent and attentive, as a Leftist Belgian deputy delivered a long and dithyrambic vindication of the French Revolution. When the European had finished, the mandarin shook his head and said, "Yes, the French Revolution was a great event, but it is still too recent. One must wait and see where it leads to, to understand it and to pass judgment on it." From the lips of this mandarin came ancient Oriental wisdom offering Europe advice which historians would do well to ponder. Precisely because the French Revolution was an event of enormous consequences, we need greater perspective to evaluate and judge its effects, which will unfold in the course of generations. If the earlier generations were satisfied with the dubious interpretations of the Right and of the Left, it was because the events were, as the Chinese mandarin pointed out, still so recent. As time passes, it will be easier for us to discover the true meaning of this great convulsion.

The major problem is to explain how the principles of the Revolution led to results that were directly opposite to those intended. The Revolution desired to preserve the monarchy, yet it decapitated the king and the members of his family. It wished to establish a government based on liberty and the right of opposition, yet the French ended up four years later under a frightful despotism. Even as it proclaimed the principle of fraternity among social classes and among all peoples, France became involved in a civil war and in a war against Europe which lasted uninterruptedly for twenty-two years, until 1814. How to explain such contradictions? By the very principles of the Revolution, respond the men of the Right, since these principles are chimerical and their application impossible. Upon reflection, such reasoning doesn't make sense. These selfsame principles which caused such disorder and contradiction in France have been implemented in other states in Europe and in America without betraying the hopes on which they were based and without resulting in wars. It remains, then, to suppose that there were in France secret, even diabolical, forces which led to these apparently absurd results. And it is the nature of these "secret" forces that we must ascertain if in truth we are to understand the French Revolution.

The word "revolution" is a word with a double meaning, a word that for the last century and a half has concealed one of the most tragic ambiguities that ever misled mankind. By "revolution" we understand at times a new orientation of the human spirit, a door opening on the future. It is in this sense that we speak of Christianity as one of the great revolutions of mankind, because it introduced the principle of the equality of men and substituted for polytheism the monotheism of the Jews. But by "revolution" we also understand the collapse or the overthrow of venerable legality, the subversion, in whole or in part, of established rules.

What is legality? It is the sum total of the laws which

establish the relationship between individuals in a society, between the governors and the governed. When it is recognized and respected, law and order reign. A legal structure is not eternal, however. For there is always a part of the population which is opposed to it. When this group rebels and seeks to destroy, there is a revolution. This is what happened in 1848 when the political and social order of half of Europe was overthrown.

There are in fact two kinds of revolutions, very different in nature: the constructive revolution and the destructive revolution. The former is always gradual, developing over centuries. The latter is always precipitate and quick. A government may be toppled in weeks, even days, as in the case of the monarchy of Louis-Philippe. Whether it brings about the downfall of a good government or of a bad government, the destructive revolution is always accompanied by a wave of fear. Fear is the inevitable baggage train of every rupture with legality. However one may dispute it, a legal government is a guarantee of stability. When it collapses, fear takes hold. The Bible recognized this profound truth: when the law falls, heaven and earth tremble.

These two forms of revolution may coexist without necessarily being tied together. An ancient legality, and its whole system of laws, can crumble without a change in the orientation of the human spirit, and there can be a new orientation of spirit without a destruction of the legal system. It is an illusion to think that it is sufficient to destroy the existing legal system in whole or in part and

8

there will immediately ensue a new order that will bring greater happiness to mankind.

When a historic accident makes both revolutions—a new orientation for mankind and the destruction of the legal fabric—coincide, there is great confusion and extraordinary complications follow. The French Revolution is the most grandiose example of an ambiguous revolution from beginning to end, because of its twofold origin. The ancient legal monarchy collapsed at the very moment that France was attempting to transform the state and society according to a new spirit. Two different revolutions—one creative, the other destructive—took place at the same time, and the destructive one weakened and led astray the creative one, ending in paralysis and annihilation. Here is the secret of the French Revolution, the key to all its contradictions.

On May 5, 1789, the Estates-General opened solemnly at Versailles. Necker made a detailed presentation of the financial situation of the kingdom. Barentin, the Keeper of the Seal, spoke in his speech of voting by head or by order. As we know, the Estates-General brought together the members of the three orders into which France was then divided: the clergy, the nobility, and the Third Estate. Should the three orders deliberate separately or together, should votes be counted by head or by order? This was the first serious problem that had to be resolved. If each order deliberated separately and exercised just one vote, the clergy and the nobility would always outvote the Third Estate, even though the Third Estate had as many deputies as the two other estates combined. The matter was of the utmost importance; that the Keeper of the Seal posed the question without giving an answer indicated that the king had left the decision up to the Assembly. He did not oppose joint deliberations or the possibility that the vote would be by head, that is, that the Estates-General would transform itself into a body akin to our modern parliaments.

At the opening session another speech was delivered, that of the king. In it he expressed a fear of too new an approach. Radical change could bring the most dire consequences. Louis XVI had good reason for apprehension.

On the following day, May 6, the three orders convened separately. By a vote of 188 to 47, the members of the nobility decided to verify their credentials separately. This was their response to the speech of the Keeper of the Seal. They indicated their desire to meet separately and to vote by order and not by head. The clergy took the same position by a vote of 133 for and 114 against. As for the Third Estate, it vainly waited for the two other orders to join it to verify their credentials in common. The Third Estate waited until 2:30 in the afternoon and then adjourned. The following days passed in negotiations aimed at reconciling the three estates. The Third Estate attempted, without success, to win over the deputies of the clergy and the nobility who had voted for deliberations in common. The government remained a disinterested spectator in the conflict. The days passed, and nothing was accomplished. The financial situation grew worse. The country was in ferment. There was an expectancy of the unusual, the extraordinary. The Estates-General, which had been convened to transform France, appeared suddenly to have become impotent. For more than a month, from May 5 to June 10, it was completely immobilized.

To what can this sudden attack of paralysis be attributed? One can speak of the selfishness of the privileged orders. But this explanation is too simple. During the indecisive discussion over the verification of credentials, a more serious problem was posed, one which no one wanted to face directly: that of the legislative power.

The Estates-General was an assembly whose origin dated back to the Middle Ages. It had no competence to reshape France since it did not possess a shred of legislative power. Its only legal justification for being was the royal convocation. It could remonstrate, advise, consent to taxation, but no more. It had been elected during a general wave of enthusiasm and had drawn up thirty-six folio volumes of proposed reforms. But these volumes could merely be placed at the feet of the king and recommended to his grace. Only the sovereign and his council had the power to enact into law the demands of the celebrated *Cahiers*. How could Louis XVI be expected to exercise the power necessary to translate these thirty-six folio volumes into reforms, when he had convoked the Estates-General precisely because he felt incapable of balancing the budget of the kingdom? It was an impossible situation.

On the eve of the Revolution the legislative power as

well as the executive power rested with the king alone. He exercised this power with the help of his ministers, whom he had chosen from the court. This power, which was concentrated ultimately in the hands of five or six persons, did not at all correspond with the vital needs of a country of twenty-five million inhabitants, the richest and most powerful nation in Europe. Living in isolation, prisoners at the court of Versailles, without any real attachment to the nation, and deprived of an adequate base for ruling, these men had neither the power nor the prestige necessary to draw up and to propose reforms.

On the one hand, there was the old, established legislative and executive power, the Royal Council, which alone had the legal authority to effect the necessary reforms but which was inadequate to the task. On the other hand, there was the imposing assembly of twelve hundred deputies which the French people, with irrepressible enthusiasm, had sent to Versailles with the mission of reforming the state, but which lacked the means to do it. The deputies had scarcely met when they were faced with the immediate necessity of profoundly modifying the existing legal system and asserting the right of legislative power. To claim this power, however, meant taking it from the king. The Estates-General was hesitant to proceed to such a destructive revolution. Hence the paralysis which seemed to overtake it. For the Third Estate was not at all, as it has been generally represented to be, a revolutionary assembly, impatient from the start to reconstruct France from top to bottom. The inaction of the Estates-General, which lasted the four weeks following the opening meeting, was an expression of its hesitation before the mighty problem of legislative power, which everyone tried to avoid while deliberating over the verification of credentials. Such a situation could not last indefinitely. The Estates-General did nothing, the court did nothing, and in the meantime France was headed for the abyss.

On June 10, one man finally took the responsibility to broach the question that everyone seemingly wanted to avoid: it was the Abbé Sieyès. He is less well known in the history of the Revolution than Robespierre, Marat, or Danton. But he played a more significant role than they did. He was a man of the Church, but he was closely associated with the secular society of his times, as were all abbots in the eighteenth century. Sieyès was a philosopher and a physician. His initiative proved decisive in two of the most important moments in the French Revolution. In 1789 he persuaded the Third Estate that it must carry out a destructive revolution, and in 1799 he planned the *coup d'état* of Brumaire, which gave rise to totalitarian government. Sieyès drew up the plan; Napoleon executed it.

On June 10, Sieyès proposed to the "People"—that was the name assumed by the Third Estate—that they organize themselves into an assembly and summon the members of the privileged orders to the meeting place of the Estates-General for a joint verification of credentials. "The Assembly considers that it is the urgent duty of all the representatives of the nation, regardless to which class of citizens they belong, to organize without delay a functioning assembly capable of instituting and fulfilling its mission." Essentially, the proposal was the claim, pure and simple, to legislative power. Though the meaning was quite explicit, the expression "functioning assembly" was purposely ambiguous. In order not to offend the king, Sieyès endeavored to hide as far as possible the revolutionary character of his proposal. "As a consequence, and because of the necessity the representatives of the nation are under to act without further delay," continued Sieyès, in addressing the members of the two privileged orders, "the deputies of the commune beseech you again, and their duty prescribes that they summon you for the last time to be present at the Hall of the Estates-General and to cooperate and to agree to a joint verification of credentials."

The expression "summon" having been found too strong, Sieyès consented to replace it by "invite." A discussion followed. At the evening session the motion was finally approved. The privileged orders having declined the invitation of the Third Estate, Sieyès on June 15 proposed that it proclaim itself the sole representative of the nation. Again the Third Estate hesitated. In the course of the discussion Mirabeau delivered a major speech. It should be quoted in its entirety. Unfortunately, its length obliges us to restrict ourselves to the following passages:

The Collapse of Monarchical Legitimacy

We must constitute ourselves as a body, on that we are all agreed. But how? In what form? Under what name? As the Estates-General? The term is improper. You all know it. It presupposes three orders, three estates. Certainly the three orders are not represented here. Has it been proposed that we constitute ourselves under another title, a synonym, after all, of the title Estates-General? I ask: will you have the sanction of the King and can you do without it? Can the authority of the King lie dormant even for an instant? Must he not concur in your decree? Is he not bound to do so? If we deny, contrary to all principles, that the King's sanction is necessary to give effect to any act of this assembly, will he accord it to subsequent laws which we must realize are not valid if they emanate from a constitution that the King will not recognize?

Are you certain of the approval of your constituents? Do not think that the people are interested in the metaphysical discussions which you have carried on until now. Undoubtedly they are of greater importance than will be given to them: they are the development and the consequence of the principles of national representation, the basis of all constitutions. But the people are still too far removed to understand the system of laws and a sound theory of liberty. The people want improvements because they have no more strength with which to suffer; they are weary of oppression because they can no longer breathe under the terrible weight that is pressing down on them; but all they ask is to pay what they can and peacefully to bear their misery. . . .

The title of deputy, known and confirmed by the French nation, suits neither your dignity nor the execution of your duties, because the meeting you would hope to be able to bring about will force you to change it. Do not take a title that

15

alarms. Look for one that no one can contest, one that is flexible but no less imposing in its magnitude, that will be suitable to all times and be susceptible to all developments which events will allow you, and may, if needed, be of use as an aid to the national laws and principles.

In my opinion, the appropriate title would be Representative of the French People. Who can dispute you this title? Will this not become the title when your principles become known, when you will have proposed good laws, when you will have gained the public confidence? What will the other two orders do then? Will they support you? It will be necessary that they do so; and if they see this necessity, will they also see that it will be easier for them to support you than to continue their opposition? Will they refuse their support? We will then speak out against them so that everyone will be able to judge between us. . . .

At this moment I am inclined to insist upon the suitability of the name that I have adopted: Representative of the French People. I say the suitability because I recognize that the motion of M. the Abbé Sieyès conforms strictly to principles, and such is to be expected from a citizen-philosopher. But, gentlemen, it is not always expedient, it is not always convenient to consider laws without regard to circumstances.

This is the essential difference between the philosopher who sits in his room deep in thought and apprehends the truth in its pristine purity, and the statesman who is obliged to take into account causes, problems, and obstacles; it is, I say, the difference between the teacher of the people and the political administrator. One thinks only of "that which is"; and the other, of "that which may be."

The metaphysician traveling the map of the world goes

*everywhere without difficulty, is hindered neither by moun-
tains nor by deserts nor by rivers or abysses; but when we
wish to make this voyage, when we seek to reach our goal,
we must always remember that it is the earth we tread on
and not an ideal world.*

The fundamental idea of Mirabeau's speech may be
summarized as follows: "Royal convocation is the only
legal authorization for your meeting and deliberations.
You cannot rebel against the king without diminishing
his power and destroying your own at the same time. Do
not count upon public opinion, it is still too fluctuating
and indecisive to absolve you! If you wish to regenerate
France and give it the new order it aspires to, strive to
weaken the legality of the monarchy as little as possible.
In other words, if you want to make a constructive revolution, be on guard against making a destructive revolution,
since it will lead to civil war, and the reforms that you
plan to institute will then not be realized." The point of
view that Mirabeau upheld is the opposite of that which
has prevailed in the Western world in the past fifty years,
which is that it is sufficient to destroy the existing legal
structure to regenerate the world. The events that followed furnished him with striking confirmation that he
was right. Mirabeau had come to the conclusion that the
legislative power could not be seized from the king by a
revolutionary act but that it was up to Louis XVI to dele-
gate this power to the Assembly by a voluntary act of
wisdom.

This speech was addressed as much to the king as to

the Assembly. In language deliberately enigmatic but sufficiently explicit, he urged Louis XVI to take the initiative in a great reform of legislative power, since it was indispensable for it to have a broader base. At the same time he recommended that the Assembly work in harmony and close cooperation with the sovereign and do everything possible to make the royal concession seem to be dictated by spontaneous good will. In this way it would appear that the royal authority, far from being diminished, had in fact been strengthened. Mirabeau gave expression to the hesitations and fears to which the Assembly was prey. Otherwise, how is he to be understood?

In the second part of the speech, Mirabeau proposed that the Third Estate substitute for the title "Representative of the Nation," which Sieyès had conferred upon it, the title "Representative of the People." The term "nation" implied France with all its classes. The term "people" underscored the idea of France to the exclusion of the privileged orders, the clergy and the nobility. If the Third Estate proclaimed, "We are the nation," that would mean that the clergy and the nobility counted for naught. But no one could contest the title of representative of the people. Here again is emphasized Mirabeau's constant preoccupation to avoid any rupture with the existing legal structure, to avoid a destructive revolution.

The discussion lasted three days. The Assembly awaited a denouement at the king's initiative, the initiative which Mirabeau had urged in veiled words. It was the last respite Louis XVI was to have to carry out the awaited

action. He could have spared France and the Western
world great disorder. But he did nothing. Who is to
blame? The king? The court? The king's ministers? No
one can say. In any event, on June 17, by a vote of 491 to
90, the Third Estate proclaimed itself the National Assembly and notified the other two estates that it would
convene, with or without their agreement. The Rubicon
had been crossed. It was inevitable. The Assembly could
not remain any longer in this state of inaction which so
irritated the masses. How would the court react? Lacking
confidence in itself, it hesitated and then adopted an
attitude of timid resistance.

On June 20, when the deputies of the Third Estate
sought to enter the chamber of the Estates-General, they
found it closed on the pretext that it was being made
ready for the plenary session. They went instead into the
tennis court and there took the famous oath not to dis-
band until they had given France a new constitution. At a
plenary session held on June 23, the three orders met with
the king and the court. Louis XVI declared unconstitu-
tional the decisions taken by the Third Estate on June 17.
He fixed narrow limits to the activity of the Assembly. He
ordered the three estates to convene separately in the hall
to which each had been assigned. If the Estates-General
disbanded, he would carry out the necessary reforms
alone. This was a grave speech. It manifested the will of
the king to maintain the restrictions on legislative power
which the nation no longer desired. The king withdrew,
but the deputies of the Third Estate remained in their

places. When the grand master of ceremonies returned and repeated the order of the king, Mirabeau replied with the well-known phrase: "We are here by the will of the people and we shall not depart except by the force of bayonets."

Logically, the court should have dispersed the Assembly by armed force. It hesitated for three days and then capitulated. On June 28, the king ordered the deputies of the clergy and the nobility to join the Third Estate. The court acceded chiefly for two reasons. First of all, the fear of bankruptcy. Second, the court was not very sure of the loyalty of the troops and even less of that of the officers. On August 9, the Estates-General proclaimed itself the Constituent Assembly. The legislative power had passed from the king to the Assembly. The legal structure had been violently disrupted. This revolution was justified: an imperious necessity had dictated it.

The revolution, once accomplished, did not arouse the enthusiasm one might have expected. In the following weeks a general uneasiness, a painful anxiety, gripped all classes of the population, as well as the Assembly and the court. Everyone seemed to sense the dangers that menaced the nation. As Mirabeau had predicted, the revolution that had triumphed on June 28 proved as disastrous for the Assembly's authority as for the king. The Assembly was incapable of transforming itself overnight into a modern parliament. Nothing had prepared it to exercise the legislative power which it had just seized. It was not yet recognized as a sovereign authority with defined powers. True, it had been elected by the unanimous will of France, with the mission of regenerating the country. But, though it was zealous, this will was exercised only on occasion and remained incoherent and confused. "Do not believe yourself supported by the will of the French people," said Mirabeau. "It is too unreliable to support you in the long and difficult task of reform."

The National Assembly could not lay claim to a royal convocation as could the Estates-General. Hereafter it would always want for this legal claim. Neither could it, after rejecting the ancient laws of the realm, find support in the traditional division of France in three classes. Inexperienced, without powers or defined rights, it lacked both the authority and the necessary means for enacting legislation. Its coup in June had placed it in an even more difficult position than the court. If the prestige of that body had been diminished, that of the king remained intact. The monarchy always enjoyed the respect and confidence of the people. Hope of an agreement between the king and the National Assembly had not been abandoned. Who knows if matters would not have turned out otherwise if two weeks later, on July 14, a catastrophe without precedent in history had not resulted in the collapse of the political, judicial, and military structure of France?

For those who for a century have exalted the French Revolution, the taking of the Bastille has been a symbol of the conquest of liberty by the people. An incorporeal giant, the people of Paris, swept along by a sublime and overwhelming emotion, rose and overthrew with one blow the ramparts of tyranny. History and legend have embroidered this episode, one of the most popular of the Revolution. But the facts are known by all. Disturbed by the spirit of revolt rampant in Paris, the court in a final burst of energy had massed troops around the capital after June 28. This aroused the National Assembly. Its recent successes, far from strengthening it, had weakened it. It feared that the precautionary measures were directed against it and requested the king to remove the troops. For its part, the court feared the Assembly and the restless Parisian masses. The ensuing discussion between the court and the Assembly provoked the masses further. On July 14, they attacked and pillaged an arms depot at the Invalides, and they stormed the Bastille. The ancient fortress did not offer any defense. After a show of resistance, it capitulated on conditions that were then not respected. The murder of Governor de Launay became the first crime of the Revolution.

The attack on the Bastille was only one of a long series of incidents which reflected the state of unrest France had fallen into: an uprising which, nonetheless, assumed great proportions, as it had turned against an ancient symbol of the Old Regime. The consequences were to be incalculable.

Scarcely had this event become known in the provinces than the ancient monarchical legality was swept away and in a few days all the organs of power were paralyzed. Barracks, monasteries, and convents were emptied; the army disintegrated, soldiers no longer obeyed officers, and the officers no longer dared issue orders to the soldiers. The police and judicial system ceased functioning. No one paid taxes. Castles, monasteries, and convents were pillaged. The peasants and the bourgeoisie carried out what Aulard has called the municipal revolution of July 1789, installing themselves as rulers in place of the ineffectual authorities. They deliberated; they organized a militia.

The sudden and total destruction of an ancient legal structure was a unique phenomenon. History offers us many examples of partial disruptions caused by disastrous wars or by civil wars; of conspiracies or coups. A destructive revolution always has as its point of departure an act of violence. But in France all this took place at a time of peace, without shocks from without, solely as a result of failure from within. And the legal structure of France was destroyed, though the central authority still remained.

An analogous event took place in Russia when the revolutionaries seized power after the abdication of Czar Nicholas II. But the collapse of Russia is more easily explained. It developed in a more rational series of steps over a period of eight months, from the abdication of the Czar in March to the coming of the Bolsheviks in November 1917. The disintegration of the army led to the disintegration of the police; that of the police to that of the judicial system; and so on. In France, it all crumbled within six weeks. In Russia the collapse had as its point of departure the abdication of the emperor, the keystone on which the entire system rested. In France the Old Regime, which rested upon the power of the monarch, fell, but the

23

king remained for three years more. In Russia it was the great war of 1914, which by overextending the forces of the Czarist empire weakened the whole regime, which set in motion the Russian Revolution. In France the downfall took place at a dizzying speed and at a time of peace.

In abstract, what happened in 1789 can easily be explained. One need only remember the definition of a government: a small, well-organized minority which imposes itself upon an unorganized majority. A government never has any difficulty with individual, isolated rebellions; it puts them down easily. But even the most powerful government must succumb before long if all its subjects simultaneously agree not to obey it. No government can resist the contagion of universal disobedience. Such a thing would seem impossible if we did not have the example of France during the six weeks which followed the capture of the Bastille, as well as of Russia in 1917. In 1789 the masses revolted and authority was paralyzed. There is an immediate and irresistible correlation: the masses revolt because they feel that authority is paralyzed, and authority ceases to act because it feels that it has lost control of the masses. Hence, catastrophe. How does this correlation come about? Only an incomplete answer is possible to this question.

It would be a major error to regard the capture of the Bastille and its consequences as a prolongation of the conflict between the court and the Estates-General. It is evident that the June "Putsch" by the Assembly, when it seized the legislative power from the king, had shaken the Old Regime. But a correlation of cause and effect cannot be established between these events and the crisis of July, since there is no common denominator between them. Such a great destruction must have a more distant cause. Was it not a consequence of the state of exhaustion the royal authority found itself in; a progressive weakening, caused by what might be called the "extravagances" of the monarchy beginning with Richelieu and Louis XIII?

That the monarchy had achieved great things is undeniable. It had transformed France into a power of a new type, which assured her of diplomatic and military hegemony in Europe, permitting her to extend her frontiers and to create a vast colonial empire. France became the showplace of the arts, after having taken from Italy its supremacy in the production of luxury goods. Such a development is witness to much imagination and great energy, but not political judgment. Is not politics the balancing of the goals one pursues with the means one employs? In France this growth of power required an effort beyond the resources of the monarchy and the country. And such was the disposition of goals and means that crimes were committed against morality, against reason, and certainly against common sense. Hence, the extravagances the effects of which were most keenly felt in the realm of finance. From the seventeenth century on, the fiscal policy of the monarchy veritably defied reason and moral sense. It sold everything, even the most sacred things: the right to work, titles of nobility, military and judicial offices. Louis XIV even sold the right to administer the municipalities. Magistrates' offices were sold and became practically the patrimonial property of individuals and could be resold without the king having a voice in the matter. By this one can gauge the weakness of the king's power, though it appeared so stately and magnificent. During the seventeenth and eighteenth centuries the courts of London, Vienna, and Berlin showed less daring and imagination but more political sense than the court of Versailles.

What was the result? To shield itself against the protests that its policies might provoke, the court early in the seventeenth century began to isolate itself, to monopolize all power, to sever its ties with the nobility, the clergy, and the *haute bourgeoisie*. The court no longer sought to work along with these classes; henceforth they served only as a source of clerks.

From this time on the king had around him only minions to execute his wishes. That is why the Estates-General was not convoked after 1614. Limited to the king and his council, the government lost all touch with the country. The political expedients to which the king resorted time and again to procure financial resources—since wars bring great expenditures—served only to increase the isolation. The government grew progressively weaker. The greater the task, the more difficult it became for the government to meet it. On the eve of the Revolution, France found herself under the rule of an apparently all-powerful absolutism—which in reality was extremely fragile, for it was no longer its own master. The moment finally came when the government no longer was capable of coping with a revolutionary movement.

Is this explanation conclusive? It seems at least to come close to the truth. Be that as it may, these are the facts: within four weeks the old legal monarchical regime had collapsed, and France was left without an army, without police, without justice, without an administration. This was the most rapid and the most complete destructive revolution that history has known: a revolution which no one had predicted, or wanted, but which over the centuries everybody, without knowing it, had been laboring to create. The entire French Revolution, with its succession of great events, springs from this collapse. The French Revolution was neither an "act of folly," as the historians of the Right say, nor the "liberation of humanity," as the historians of the Left say, but a desperate effort to create a new legal system to replace the one that was destroyed in the four weeks following the taking of the Bastille. It was to require twenty-five years to achieve that. Twenty-five years of blood spilled in torrents, of revolutions and wars without number! The enormity of the effort and the complexity of events prevented the recognition of the goal for which they were striving. But this goal never changed. Considered from this point of view, the Revolution ceases to be a monster or a wonder. It becomes, in all its complications, an event in the progress of man which is perfectly understandable and highly instructive. It shows us how easy it is to destroy and how difficult it is to rebuild a legal structure. Twenty-five years to rebuild what was destroyed in four weeks!

With the collapse of the ancient legitimate monarchy there began the Great Fear, which helps explain what happened first in France and then in Europe. Historians have studied this strange collective psychosis which seized the masses after the capture of the Bastille and which took very different forms in different regions.

The Fear took hold not only of the peasants, the workers, and the petty bourgeoisie, but of all the social classes; of the court as of the Assembly, the people, the nobility, and the clergy. Great and humble, rich and poor, wise and ignorant, all trembled together, now that the pillar of society, the law, had been overthrown. It was a general terror which multiplied the real dangers by every kind of imaginary danger and created a veritable delirium of fright. In the countryside the peasants took up arms to repulse imaginary brigands. The news spread from place to place: "They are coming, they are coming!" In a panic, the bourgeoisie armed themselves, too, and in various towns declared a state of siege. There was talk of the arrival of a foreign army supported by the princes; of an underground plot by the aristocracy. At the same time many people took to the roads in flight. The plot and the foreign invaders were no less imaginary than the brigands. The noblemen, frightened by the growing anarchy and aware that the government was no longer functioning, began to flee into exile before an as yet nonexistent danger, a danger which their very flight was to advance. The brother of the king set the example. The fear was two-fold: the upper classes feared the masses, and the masses feared the upper classes. Attributing to each other the same hostile intentions, both took to flight. Both feared the general anarchy which they had together produced. The masses, terrified by the anarchy they had created, began to revolt everywhere, attacking castles, burning the records, and refusing to pay taxes. And the upper classes, terrified as well, offered no resistance and fled into exile.

One must know what a revolution is to understand the terror of those who have lost the protection of the law and who feel themselves at the mercy of dangers and capricious forces they do not and can not recognize. Most histories of the French Revolution were written between 1814 and 1914—a period in which, except for a few years, Europe lived in order and peace. It was difficult then to envision a society given over to a permanent state of fear, in which life becomes impossible and the most reasonable men commit the most foolish acts.

CHAPTER 2
The Constituent Assembly

At the very outset the Constituent Assembly was most energetic in enacting legislation. In a few months it made a clean sweep of the Old Regime. It abolished the last vestiges of feudalism, class distinctions, the sale of public offices, commercial and industrial monopolies, the special privileges of the market towns and of the provinces, and finally it abolished the *Parlements* which had been the cause of so much trouble to the kings. At the same time the Constituent Assembly approved a series of laws that gave France a new direction. It was indeed a constructive revolution, audacious and magnificent in what it was about to accomplish. Yet all this work was to end in frightful chaos: in the Terror. Hence the opposing judgments passed on its accomplishments.

For the historians of the Right, the National Constituent Assembly provoked the catastrophe by its frenetic revolutionary activity, by thinking that the life of a country could be recast merely by passing new laws. Such a chimerical conception must inevitably lead to legislation that has neither historic nor social nor psychological basis.

The historians of the Left maintain, on the other hand, that the work of the Assembly represented a magnificent attempt to create, by sheer will and intelligence, a rational order designed to assure the happiness of mankind. If this effort was not crowned with the success it promised, the fault rests with the Conservatives, all those whose interests remained tied to the Old Regime and who diligently applied themselves to running the revolution to the ground.

In reality, it is the Great Fear which alone can explain the state of mind of the Constituent Assembly. It was amid widespread fear and anarchy that the Assembly, beginning in August 1789, was obliged to legislate. Hence the contradiction between the spirit that inspired the passage of these laws and the results they produced.

What is a legislative assembly? An assembly of persons who discuss legislation designed to assure the welfare of the state. When there is free discussion—and freedom of discussion is the first prerequisite—two possibilities arise. Either everyone is in agreement and there are no problems, or there are disagreements and the assembly is divided into a majority and a minority. Opposition, although by a minority, is necessary. It constitutes a limitation of the powers of the majority, which may not be exceeded without the risk of a breakup of the assembly. This is why a representative government is so far superior to other forms of government.

If at Versailles the National Assembly had been able to deliberate under normal conditions, two parties would have formed: on the Left, a revolutionary party which would have demanded radical reforms; and on the Right, a conservative party which would have endeavored to limit acts of a destructive nature and to prevent a too rapid turn in political direction. The conservative party would have included the great majority of the nobility, the upper clergy, and the rich bourgeoisie. If the Right had been in the majority, the revolutionary minority would have forced it to carry out a certain number of indispensable reforms. If the Left had been in the majority, the conservative minority would have kept it from altogether destroying the past and from going too far in reconstructing the present. It would have acted as a braking force. Under either condition, the minority would have played a vital role. But because of the Great Fear, the conservative forces were disorganized and almost completely eliminated, and only the revolutionary forces remained.

The collapse of monarchical legitimacy paralyzed the court, and the conservative forces which depended on it found themselves reduced to impotence. After August, the king was, in effect, a sovereign without power. He no longer possessed any machinery of government. He had no administration, no judicial system, no army, no treasury. Most of his agents had abandoned him. Most of the nobility retired to their estates or fled into exile. So weakened, the Right no longer had the courage to defend itself against the revolutionary party, which, after July, appeared to have won a decisive victory.

These events had immediate repercussions in the Assembly. A considerable number of the deputies of the nobility, of the upper clergy, and even of the Third Estate disappeared during the great disorders following the fall of the Bastille. From week to week, the number of those who attended the Assembly became smaller and smaller. Of twelve hundred representatives, not more than five or six hundred remained. The elimination of the conservative elements strengthened the position of the revolutionary group and increased its power. It no longer had any obstacles to overcome. Every rash law that was proposed was approved without opposition. Finally it became so easy to rule, once the established legal system was abolished, that it was inevitable that France would be remade from top to bottom.

The twofold necessity of creating a new legal system and of dispersing the conservative forces explains the great number of laws passed in so short a time. When it came to enforcing them, however, the difficulties began. The Great Fear had destroyed not only the opposition in the Assembly but also the executive power, and the new laws remained dead letters or, at best, were only partially implemented.

Among the new laws should be cited first of all the

Declaration of the Rights of Man and the Citizen. It was one of the most important acts of the Assembly, for it revealed in striking form the aspirations for a new direction for the state and for society which French writers and philosophers had given voice to for a century. In heralding the coming reign, not of fear but of reason, of liberty, equality, and fraternity, the Declaration of the Rights of Man was a gate grandly opened to the future, one of the greatest monuments in the history of mankind. Consider, incidentally, the second article, which cites "property" as one of the natural rights of man. Taking "property" to be what we understand today as capitalism, the socialists find confirmation here for what they call the bourgeois character of the Revolution. This is a serious error in historical perspective. The Assembly only wanted to protect property against the abuses of power by the monarchy; there had been innumerable abuses of this nature in the preceding two centuries, especially during the campaigns against the Protestants, when confiscations multiplied. To prevent a repetition of such abuses, the Constituent Assembly declared that property was a natural and inalienable right of man.

Let us not forget the situation France was in during the discussion and vote on the Declaration of Rights. One gets an idea of it from the picture drawn by the Archbishop of Bordeaux in a speech delivered to the Assembly on August 7: property violated, dwellings ravaged, commerce and industry paralyzed, justice ignored, unrestrained license, law without authority. Necker declared that taxes were not being paid, that toll stations were being pillaged, their account books scattered, etc. Under the circumstances, a proclamation of martial law to reestablish law and order was clearly more necessary than a metaphysical charter of the rights of man! How could such a charter be implemented in the midst of such terrible disorder, with the executive arm of government completely disorganized and the people terrified? These rights could not be enforced, and they were not enforced, not by any of the four governments that sprang from the Revolution: the Convention, the Directory, the Consulate, and the Empire. The tragedy of the Revolution was that it was unable to carry out the principles it proclaimed. What was the reason? Fear. Only with the restoration of the monarchy, when order was finally reestablished in France, did these rights cease to be purely fictitious. If between 1814 and 1914 Europe lived in a state of peace, it was due in part to the principles of the Declaration, which were applied to some degree in all countries, and even influenced legislation in absolute monarchies.

What a strange state of affairs for the Assembly! Its situation can be defined as impotent omnipotence. The Assembly could make laws but could not enforce them. And this was not the only contradiction. The Assembly might also be called timorously bold: daring in the theoretical, timid when it came to practical matters. For the Constituent Assembly was afraid. It was afraid of the discontent that its reforms had created among the members of the Old Regime, the court, the clergy, the nobility, and

35

the high bourgeoisie. As seductive as its new orientation might appear at first glance, it could not fail to injure the interests of many and to frighten many, especially when it began to become a concrete fact. The discontent of the upper classes was in itself of little account. The upper classes, too, were afraid and completely disorganized; their opposition was practically meaningless.

The Assembly was nonetheless afraid. Having so recently come into being and still unsure of its right to legislate, the Assembly was uncertain of itself. It saw itself as isolated in the midst of general anarchy and without an army to defend it. The discontent of the upper classes grew in proportion to the reforms that were passed. Fear was reciprocally generated. The court, the nobility, and the clergy feared the Assembly, which in turn feared them. Each act, even the most innocent, was interpreted by the other faction as hostile to itself. To these tendentious interpretations were added accusations of imaginary conspiracies. The National Assembly also feared the restlessness of the masses in the larger cities, chiefly in Paris. These mobs were prey to a veritable delirium of persecution, attributing all their sufferings to plots on the part of the court and the higher clergy.

In the midst of the general anarchy, such frenzy was indeed dangerous, for the mobs ruled the streets, free to demonstrate as they wished and when they wished, on any pretext whatever. In Paris, the most turbulent city in France, the majority of the people remained peaceful and resigned, with no idea or desire to revolt against the secular arm of government. Who profited the most from the newly proclaimed right to demonstrate? A small minority that sincerely believed that the court was responsible for the poverty and enforced idleness of the people. The rule of the streets by this minority, violent, full of hate, and obsessed with a delirium of persecution, was to become a formidable instrument for acts against authority. Indeed, the irreparable measures that would throw France into civil war were enacted under pressure from this minority.

On August 27 the Assembly approved the Declaration of the Rights of Man and the Citizen, and in September the constitutional laws that would give France a new political orientation. This constitution was not fashioned all at once. Indeed, it was not voted on until two years later. But its principal articles were enacted in September 1789. On the first of October they were sent to the king, along with the Declaration of Rights, for his ratification. These articles, nineteen in number, were the cornerstone of the future constitution. They laid down important principles: that France was a monarchy; that the person of the king was inviolable; that the executive power rested with him—with the absolute right to choose or dismiss his ministers. The legislative power was entrusted to a permanent assembly, but the king had a suspensive veto over all decisions taken by the assembly. This was recognition that he should be a moderating force on the majority. The prudence and sagacity of this action is manifest, and submission to royal authority became the keystone of the political and social order. But the nineteen articles contained a gap, which Louis XVI at once pointed out in a letter read to the Assembly on October 15. To attribute executive power to the monarch was of no value if, given the anarchy that prevailed, the Assembly would not help restore the power of the sovereign.

The historians of the Left have denounced this letter as a form of treason, as proof of the king's hostility toward the Assembly and the principles of the Revolution. Such an accusation is groundless. Louis XVI, with much good sense, said, in substance: "What you have offered me is fine. Do not forget, however, that there is no police, no justice, no army, no order, and since all commerce has ceased, Paris is in danger of starvation. If you recognize my executive powers, give me the means to exercise them." The king was right. The Declaration of Rights and the nineteen articles resolved the most urgent of all problems, that of executive power, only on paper. He was right, but the Assembly took a dim view of his letter.

The king himself was all that remained of the ancient monarchical legal system. If the Assembly showed him respect, it was in order to gain, through him, support for the new constitution. But after assigning executive power to the king, the Assembly was afraid to give him the means to exercise it. Indeed, the masses were more and more paranoiac, which they manifested often and violently, mainly in Paris, toward all measures for augmenting the power of the court and of the king. Therein they saw a menace to their liberty and livelihood; they protested that such power would only be used to restore the people to their former bondage. Those who knew how to excite the popular passions, profiting from the freedom of the press, began their work. The question of the veto power provoked great agitation in Paris, which deeply disturbed the Constituent Assembly. Lacking a solid legal base, the Assembly was all the more frightened by this anti-royalist psychosis—which led to a strange episode: the abduction of the royal family by a mob of women.

Paris had become the center of the luxury industries, assuring France of an unchallenged primacy since the seventeenth century. Its customers were the court, the nobility, and the Church. The Church, especially, bought enormous quantities of art objects and luxury goods. But the Revolution swept away the court, impoverished the nobility, and ruined the Church. Hence the unemployment crisis and the miserable state of the working class. The crisis finally passed because in a few years the nobility resumed its spending, the new rich built great homes, and vast markets were opened in the conquered territories.

The crisis began in the autumn of 1789. It was further complicated by shortages, for the harvest had been bad and transportation was inadequate. Added to this was a scarcity of bread in Paris. The enthusiastic minority that favored revolution explained the economic difficulties to suit itself. If there was no work and no bread, the fault lay with the court, the nobility, and the clergy, who wished to punish the people and the Assembly for supporting the Revolution. It was even said that the Archbishop of Paris had paid the millers to stop their mills and starve the people. It was amid this ferment that a procession of women arrived at Versailles on October 5 and invaded the Assembly demanding bread. The Assembly lacked the courage to repulse them with bayonets. The women were directed to the king and were accompanied by a delegation which sought to profit by the occasion to demand ratification of the Declaration of Rights and the nineteen articles. After a long interview, the king promised to ratify the measures. As for bread, since none was to be had, he could not give any. The women remained at Versailles all night and were joined by thousands of men. The following morning the crowd invaded the palace, seized the royal family, and brought it that afternoon to Paris. Several days later, the Assembly joined them there.

The abduction of the court by a mob of women is one of the most mysterious episodes of the Revolution. Judging by the consequences, it would appear that this event was not spontaneous but premeditated. But by whom? By the secret societies? They had worked the most to give France a new political orientation by overthrowing the ancient legal structure. But how was it that the court, which still had a certain military force, was not able to prevent this supreme extravagance, this triumph of anarchy? Whatever the reason, in the face of this petticoat revolt the Assembly showed itself as feeble as the court. It dared not make a move against the fury of the mob. Terrified, the Assembly allowed itself to be led docilely to Paris after the court, and, more dangerous still, it submitted to the pressure of the rioters.

Yet this Assembly, so weak in the face of a revolt of women, was immensely bold with regard to the past. Scarcely had it been installed in Paris than it voted the most revolutionary of laws: a law that did away with sixteen centuries of history, destroying in one swoop one of the most ancient institutions, one of the most venerable, and one of the seemingly most inviolable of the Old Regime. This move was inspired by the enigmatic Revolutionary Charles-Maurice de Talleyrand-Périgord, Bishop of Autun, who on October 10 proposed to transfer all Church property to the state; henceforth the state would assume all religious expenses.

To understand the full import of this proposal, one must remember that on the eve of the Revolution the Catholic Church was the most powerful economic and social force. The Church possessed enormous riches, in land, real estate, gold, silver, precious metals, art objects, rents, mortgages, etc. The Church also enjoyed a privileged position legally. Its property was not subject to the communal law. It benefited from special legislation which in fact made its property inalienable. This immense wealth made the Church a political power and assured it of independence not only with respect to the state but also as regards the faithful, since it did not depend on their offerings to subsist. The great part of this wealth belonged to the religious orders, which cast a tight network over the social life of the Catholic countries. Monasticism as an institution was even older than the monarchy, and it had a thousand branches. Its numerous activities included primary and secondary education, scholarship, works of charity, even certain industries, as in Italy, for example, the pastry business. The Church was a sovereign power, a veritable state within a state.

Talleyrand sought to abolish this power by a stroke of the pen. On the day that the state took over the finances of religion, the Church, till then independent, would become simply a spiritual power under state control. Its historical position would be completely changed and monasticism would be dealt a death blow. Deprived of its wealth, it would be deprived of its power. The project involved the complete secularization of society.

How was the immense wealth that the Revolution intended to strip the Church of to be utilized? For the most secular purpose of all. It was to make good the deficit that the Revolution had increased. After the seizure of the Bastille, no one paid taxes, and this tax strike, which continued into October 1789, made the need for money all the more intense. The immobility of Church property, which was for the most part poorly managed, had occasioned strong criticism for more than fifty years and was a grave problem in all Catholic countries—a problem unknown in Protestant countries.

Many programs of reform had been conceived, but Talleyrand's surpassed them all in its boldness, for it heralded a twofold revolution: the overthrow of the existing legal system and a new orientation for humanity. There was no lack of opposition to this program. The opposition was of three kinds: (1) opposition by interested parties—the higher clergy and businessmen who prospered because of the luxuries of the Church; (2) opposition by devout Catholics, for whom Church property was sacred, looked upon as the property of God on earth; (3) opposition by those who had reservations not of a religious but of a legal and moral nature. How could such a sweeping confiscation be reconciled with the Declaration of the Rights of Man, which proclaimed the inviolability of property? The contradiction was flagrant. And it had not escaped Talleyrand's attention. He denied that what he intended was confiscation. According to him, the property of the Church did not belong to any one entity, but was donated to further certain ends. The Church would lose its justification for holding property when the state assumed its functions.

Talleyrand endeavored to establish that the secularization of this wealth fulfilled the true intentions of those who had left it to the Church. The state would assure the clergy of an honest livelihood, and it would not touch their personal property. It would undertake the upkeep of churches, hospitals, and charities; the nation would carry out the will of the donors. This argument was ingenious. In reality, the state proposed to reduce the allotment for religion in order to use the wealth of the Church to restore its own finances.

On November 2, Talleyrand's motion, seconded by Mirabeau, was approved by a vote of 568 to 346, with 40 abstentions. By October, nearly two hundred deputies were no longer participating in the work of the Assembly, having emigrated. These were for the most part members

43

of the clergy and the higher aristocracy, who would probably have voted against the measure. Their absence facilitated the victory of their opponents. Because of its bold character, Talleyrand's motion gained the favor of the most revolutionary members of the Assembly. Was it not the only solution for warding off the financial crisis? The project also had the support of dissenting minorities. In the eighteenth century, France was, by a large majority, a Catholic country. But it also included influential minorities: Jews and Protestants, who were quite numerous despite persecutions; freethinkers; disciples of the Encyclopaedists and of Voltaire; Jansenists, who saw in this project the means to restore the Church to simpler ways. There were also those who rebelled against the Church, those who had taken orders against their will. Under the Old Regime the laws of inheritance condemned the younger members of great families, and especially the women, to enter the Church. Leading this rebellion was Talleyrand himself. Although the eldest in his family he was barred from a military career because of his limp, and had thus been forced to take vows. This was his revenge.

Still another factor intervened in his favor, and most decisively: the popular demonstrations organized by the revolutionary party in the Assembly. It was at this time that the actions of the minority rulers of the streets of Paris came to the foreground. They alone demonstrated. The conservative elements dared not stir and no one thought of organizing them. When the Assembly convened at Versailles, the conservatives were unable to exert a direct influence on it. The demonstrations against the veto power, when the question was under discussion in September, had, however, an effect. After its transfer to Paris, the Constituent Assembly was more and more subject to outside influence. The demonstrators entered the Assembly, applauding the revolutionary orators, interrupting and reviling the others. Were these demonstrations sufficient to secure the passage of Talleyrand's motion into law? No one can say for sure. But it is indisputable that for the first time this minority exerted pressure in a most forceful fashion. The "secularization law" would bring the Assembly further along the revolutionary path and augment the political power of the revolutionary minority in Paris.

To free itself of this influence, the Assembly would have had to ally itself with the king and reestablish a military force. But it was loath to form such an alliance. It did not wish to strengthen royal power, not because it mistrusted Louis XVI personally but because it mistrusted the court and the higher clergy. It was forced therefore to depend on the masses, who more and more were inclined to excesses. The more revolutionary laws the Assembly voted which displeased the king and his entourage, the more favored it was by the masses: they saw in it a protection against the conspiracy, real or imaginary, which they felt menaced them. This explains the huge contradictions of the Assembly and why it approved, alternately, laws that showed great wisdom and laws that were extremely revolutionary, such as the one proposed

45

by Talleyrand, which doubtlessly was dictated by financial necessity but which was nevertheless immensely reckless.

The Assembly afterward passed another law that both prudently and boldly resolved one of the most serious problems it faced in its efforts to reorganize society and the state: a masterpiece that showed its great wisdom and demonstrated that it could indeed free itself of its fear. This was the law that organized the legislative power and the electoral body that would elect the future assembly of France.

Article 3 of the Declaration of the Rights of Man set down the principle that all sovereignty rested in the nation and that no body or individual could exercise authority which did not expressly emanate from it. But how to implement this sovereignty? What kind of legislative assembly was it to be vested in? The question was all the more serious since Rousseau, the great theoretician of democracy, whom the Revolution had adopted, offered no solution to the problem. The *Social Contract* never spoke of the nation but of the people, and without defining the term. This omission was not accidental. Had he given a definition of "the people," Rousseau knew well that he would have become involved in interminable controversies. The Assembly could not let this question remain unanswered, however, and it resolved it in an original and sensible fashion, the merit of which historians have not fully appreciated, perhaps because the solution could only be temporary.

The Assembly divided citizens into two classes: passive

citizens and active citizens. Passive citizens had the right to protection of their persons and their property, if they had any, but did not have the right to take an active part in the government. These were women, men under twenty-five, and those who did not possess sufficient property to meet the requirements. The active citizens, who could participate in the government, consisted of all other citizens who paid taxes equivalent, locally, to three days' labor. Meeting in assemblies, they chose electors from among citizens paying a direct tax valued at ten days' labor. This assembly of electors in turn chose the deputies to the National Assembly and the members of the assemblies of the departments and the districts. The deputies could be chosen only from among the landed who paid a tax of at least one silver mark (a coin of 8 ounces or .2448 kilogram [old weight]).

This was suffrage in two degrees, a system dear to the Revolution. It consisted in not allowing the masses direct contact with the government, but rather establishing an intermediary between the two. The masses elected an assembly which in turn elected other assemblies. It was the Revolution which sought for the first time to apply this plan in a systematic manner. The active citizens numbered about 4,300,000. In a country of twenty-five million inhabitants and at a time when women were excluded from politics, the electoral base was quite large. Nevertheless, the historians of the Left have always been critical of this constitution. Aulard said it was not democratic but bourgeois.

To judge it properly, we must place it in the context

of the time in which it was voted. It did assure the participation of the masses in large enough numbers so that the principle of popular sovereignty was not a deception. It represented real progress over the Old Regime in the organization of legislative power. It might be censured for not taking into account education, but education was closely linked to wealth. In 1789, in an age when European society was essentially aristocratic, could more be asked of France? Proof that this constitution was sufficiently democratic lies in the fact that no recriminations were raised against it by the masses. Though they protested against the royal veto, they did not manifest opposition to the constitution. Aulard called it bourgeois because it rejected the principle of universal suffrage. But only five deputies, including Robespierre, proposed universal suffrage. Of the five revolutionary constitutions, only one granted universal suffrage; that was the one voted by the Legislative Assembly on August 11, 1792, which led to the election of the Convention. In the nineteenth century, universal suffrage was the cause of all internal political crises. How could the eighteenth century, when hierarchical society was at its height, have resolved the problem? The constitution that was voted by the Assembly was inspired by a profound sense of realism, notwithstanding the thought of the historians of the Right, who accuse the Revolution of pursuing fantasies. Indeed, if these laws proved inapplicable, it was not because of any inherent defects in them but because of two laws that were voted shortly thereafter. These two laws, which constitute an irreparable mistake on the part of the National Assembly and which undermined the Revolution, were the law dealing with administrative assemblies and the law of the Civil Constitution of the Clergy.

The chief problem still to be resolved was that of the executive power. The Assembly was afraid, but it could not evade the problem indefinitely. In September it had left the power in the hands of the king. He named the ministers, who in turn named the officials. But the law on administrative assemblies which was voted in December took back this power and transferred it to the people, that is, to the active citizens. It placed Louis XVI and his ministers in an equivocal position. Nominally, the king retained the executive power, which in the mind of the populace left him with all his former responsibilities, but he had been deprived of all means of exercising this power. The centralized monarchy was destroyed. It was henceforth up to the people to elect the agents of government. The conferring of extensive prerogatives to councils based on popular suffrage created a form of self-government on an elective basis. That was too great an innovation. It required of the active citizens an effort for which they were not prepared.

The ancient monarchy had made no demands of its citizens other than the payment of taxes. That was its great convenience. Representative government calls for personnel capable of setting in motion the complicated machinery of elections. France lacked such personnel. This was more serious still because of another factor. A

representative government such as that formulated by
the National Assembly cannot function without a strong,
stable legal order. To make and implement the laws, the
people choose men they have confidence in. This choice
cannot be real, however, unless it is free. And liberty is
not possible without an authority that safeguards it. In
disorder, men fight instead of discussing, and the supposed will of the people ends up being confused with that
of small armed bands that impose themselves by violence.
At the end of 1789, France was plunged into disorder;
public power had failed. Men stole, they pillaged with
impunity. The general anarchy constituted an insurmountable difficulty to the implementation of the constitution.

Under the monarchical regime, order had been a gift
granted from above, that is, from the king. The Assembly
sought to create a power capable of imposing it, and the
task was entrusted to the people. Every citizen was to
dress in uniform and be on guard to maintain public
order. This was the National Guard, the weaknesses of
which Taine has exposed, along with its incompetence
and the lack of authority of its leaders. The morale of the
people of France must also be considered. The reforms
that had been instituted had injured certain interests,
aroused mistrust, sowed the seeds of discord between
social classes, between rich and poor, nobles and com-
moners. Fear on both sides made any regular, permanent
association between these groups more and more difficult.

If the Assembly had its admirers who went so far as to

declare the new constitution divine, the incredulous who doubted its work grew more numerous. These things did not favor the implementation of the constitution. Immediate proof of this comes in the first departmental elections held at the beginning of 1790. All France had participated enthusiastically in the election of the Estates-General; one year later the abstentions were considerable. Only a ninth of the registered electors voted. The masses were not interested in a new government which they did not understand. Did such a limited vote confer upon the elected the right to rule as the law prescribed? By what claim of legitimacy could they justify themselves before the people?

Could those who received 150 votes out of 2,000 claim to represent the general will? Since the upper classes had abstained, the majority of those elected were from the middle class. What personal prestige did they have, to govern in a society as aristocratic as France?

It is not enough to point out the faults of this constitution; we must seek out the cause of these weaknesses. The first was the revolutionary mystique that had taken hold of the Assembly after the fall of the Bastille. The overthrow of the ancient legal structure had paralyzed the upper classes, which might have acted as a party of the Right, as a brake on the innovating tendencies of the Left. The revolutionary party, which sought to carry the new experiments to an extreme, found itself, in effect, master of the situation. Contrary to the ancient order of things, it was now enough that a new idea be proposed

for it to be received with favor. And all opposition to reforms was regarded as a culpable act of adherence to an
outdated regime that was condemned to disappear. This
was the spirit prevailing in the Assembly.

A second cause of the weakness of the constitution, and
more important even than the first, was, as we have
remarked, the Constituent Assembly's mistrust of the
court and the upper classes. This mistrust was simply a
manifestation of the universal fear that we must not lose
sight of. Otherwise the Revolution becomes a drama devoid of sense, played by drunken actors, such as Hamlet
speaks of. The upper classes were discontented and the
Assembly knew it. If for the moment these classes were
paralyzed, they would one day be able to act, and the
Assembly was afraid. The simplest way to restore order
would have been to give the king the means of doing so.
Had he not performed this function for centuries? But
this meant placing an armed force at his disposal, and
the Assembly was afraid that it would one day be used
against them. Besides, it preferred another solution, one
which required an effort on the part of the people for
which they were, however, not prepared. In America, it
was thirty years before the executive power was entrusted
to the people. This system worked well. It miscarried in
France because of the great disorder brought about by
the destructive revolution against the ancient legal system.

The complete contradiction between the two revolutions is clearly evident here: one revolution giving a new
direction to the human spirit; the other revolution destroy-

ing the existing legal framework. The second rendered the legislative actions of the first revolution much easier but made it impossible to implement the new laws. The Assembly had no difficulty in translating into law and decrees even the boldest ideas, because all resistance disappeared with the overthrow of ancient monarchical legitimacy. The laws remained up in the air, however, with no possibility of serious application, because with the downfall of ancient legality the elements of primordial order had disappeared. Amid the general anarchy it became impossible to lay the foundations of a new order, though the plan had been admirably drawn up by the Assembly. All its efforts brought only increasing disorder. This tragic contradiction was accentuated as the last resistances of the past crumbled. So it was that the omnipotence—purely theoretical—of the Constituent Assembly led to a kind of extremist frenzy that brought it to its second irreparable error: the Civil Constitution of the Clergy, passed on July 12, 1790.

The law of secularization had despoiled the Church of its riches. It had aroused strong discontent because it injured economic and financial interests, but it was not an attack against the spiritual authority of the Church. This was not so with the Civil Constitution of the Clergy, which took from the king the power to appoint bishops and gave it to the people. Under the Old Regime, investiture was only by the Pope. In authorizing a bishop in office to consecrate a priest chosen by the people, the new constitution robbed the Pope of his power as supreme

53

head of the Church. The great majority of the French people were devout, and after the condemnation of the constitution by Rome, they could no longer regard as legitimate the bishops so consecrated or the curés ordained by these bishops. The actions of those clergymen were, in the eyes of the people, a profanation, and the sacraments which this clergy administered, a sacrilege. The Civil Constitution of the Clergy violated the freedom of conscience. No worse violence could be committed than that of imposing false priests on the people.

How could the Assembly that had passed the Declaration of the Rights of Man approve the Civil Constitution of the Clergy? The influence of the anti-Catholic minority undoubtedly carried great weight, but it was not in itself decisive. It was fear, once again, which moved the Assembly: fear of the higher clergy whom the Revolution had alienated through the laws of secularization; fear of the influence they might have on the lower clergy; fear that one day the Church would mobilize against the Revolution. For the clergy was more powerfully organized than the nobility, and it obeyed a foreign power, the Pope. The Pope's influence over the people was still considerable. He was, or seemed to be, a formidable enemy. The Assembly attempted through this law to sever the bonds that linked the Church to Rome and to organize an episcopate loyal to the Revolution. This reform recalls the reform instituted by Henry VIII of England.

The Anglican Church was in fact nationalized Christianity, with the king substituting for the Pope. But France was never able to establish a national church. The attempt

The Constituent Assembly

failed because it was undertaken, not by the king or by a strong government during a time of order, but by a weak assembly that tried to institute this reform along with many others. We must also remember that during the time of Henry VIII the papacy found itself in a very difficult situation, having had to struggle with a large part of Europe which followed the doctrines of Luther. At the time that France wanted to become independent of Rome, no one in Europe was any longer concerned with this. In voting for the Civil Constitution of the Clergy, the Assembly sought to prevent a purely imaginary danger. The Civil Constitution of the Clergy only served to furnish the Pope and the faithful with a cause for protest, which the laws of secularization had not. Even the lower clergy, which for the most part had been won over to the side of the Revolution, could not accept a constitution that interfered with the tenets of the Church. The Assembly had sought to protect itself against a possible hidden danger; fear conjured up the most threatening perils.

The new constitution placed the Catholics in an impossible situation. To assume public office, active citizens had to take an oath that engaged them to accept all innovations of the Revolution, including the Civil Constitution of the Clergy. The majority of practicing Catholics renounced all political activity. The desire to provide a broader base for legislative and executive powers had justified the Revolution. Now the Revolution itself was to destroy its own work by causing the abstention of a large number of citizens who might have filled public office.

The new constitution was to have another, even more

serious, consequence. It brought to the surface the latent conflict between the Revolution and the king. Louis XVI had been waiting for an opportunity to collaborate in all sincerity with the Revolution. But he refused to approve the Civil Constitution of the Clergy and for the first time used his right of veto. The king was a good Catholic and acted out of personal conviction, but also because it was his duty to defend the sovereignty of the people, for the majority of the nation had not approved the Civil Constitution of the Clergy, which violated freedom of conscience. If ever the intervention of the king was justified, this was such a case. The constitution had been passed by intimidation, under pressure of a revolutionary minority and the threats of an unruly mob. The right of veto had been granted to the king to prevent the abuse of power by a parliamentary majority. Never had a majority abused its power so flagrantly; and a wholly artificial majority at that. In this instance Louis XVI rendered a service less to the Church than to the Revolution itself by preventing it from engaging in a great conflict with the religious authorities. This veto was to involve the king in a critical conflict with the Assembly, the epilogue of which, in 1793, would be the execution of the royal family.

The establishment of the veto was a first attempt to lay the foundations of the right of opposition in France. This right, which existed in England, was the great innovation which the Revolution proposed to introduce in the public life of France. Its exercise depended upon freedom of the press and freedom of opinion, to which the Revolution had added the royal veto. This first experience with the right of opposition was deceptive. The Assembly should have yielded to the veto of the king, but it rebelled against him. It pretended that Louis XVI had abused his power. And it was encouraged by the press, which in Paris led the campaign against the court, the higher clergy, and the nobility. Daily it denounced the progress of the counterrevolution, the headquarters of which were at court, and the dangers which threatened the work of the Assembly. This campaign of intimidation was directed competently and with great energy, so that a month and a half later, after much hesitation, the king finally capitulated. On August 24, 1790, he promulgated the Civil Constitution of the Clergy. The right of opposition had failed. The Revolution which had proclaimed it neither recognized it nor was able to put it into effect. The glory of being the first to have respected it belongs to Louis XVI—a fact that no historian, not even the most royalist, has remarked upon until now.

The flight of the king and the royal family was already being planned. Louis XVI was opposed to it; he understood its implications. But the queen and her entourage prepared to carry it out. The plan became known, however, before it could be executed. On June 6, 1791, fifteen days before the planned flight to Varennes, the *Ami du Peuple* published a long article in the form of a letter signed: "a patriot who has passed himself off as an aristocrat to save the people" (he was probably Marat). He spoke of the pressures the queen, who was called simply

Antoinette, had put on Louis XVI to convince him to flee. There was no trace of respect for the royal family. This is far indeed from the sentiments of devotion and reverence shown by the Estates-General when it convened in 1789. Things had changed considerably in two years. This letter gives us a measure of the perilous straits in which Louis XVI found himself; one can understand why he was finally won over to the plan of escape. On June 20 he left Paris secretly with his family, heading toward the eastern frontier. At news of this, the Assembly was thrown into a panic. What would happen to the country without its king, the symbol of all authority? Even if Louis XVI no longer exercised any real power, he nevertheless continued to represent, in the eyes of the people, order, the state, France. And he could not be succeeded by one of his brothers, as both had emigrated.

The Assembly was also afraid that the king might be preparing an attempt against France. It was beginning to be uneasy about the impression that the Revolution had produced in Europe. The Assembly knew of the intrigues of the émigrés with the German princes and their efforts to convince other European royalty that what was taking place in France could have grave repercussions in all the courts of Europe.

The Assembly was split in two. The moderate majority realized that it had allowed the king to be discredited; it was seized by a kind of remorse and wished to attempt a political reconciliation. There was also an extremist revolutionary minority that denounced Louis XVI as a traitor, seeking to abolish the monarchy altogether. On June 21, the word "republic" was uttered for the first time.

Louis XVI and his family, recognized and arrested at Varennes, were returned under strong guard to Paris. The failure of the attempted escape strengthened the majority that labored to acquit the king. The minority which demanded the deposition of the king had recourse to its usual methods of intimidation, which had been so successful up to now. It urged that the question of executive power be settled by the people and fomented a popular disturbance that ended in the fusillade of July 17. That day a demonstration was staged at the Champ-de-Mars. Two men who had been in hiding were discovered by the demonstrators, were branded as enemies of the people, and were murdered. On this occasion the authorities found the necessary energy to intervene. Lafayette, the head of the National Guard, marched on the Champ-de-Mars and ordered that the rioters be fired upon. The disturbance ceased immediately; for the first time the moderates had triumphed.

After the flight to Varennes the Assembly suspended the king's powers and assumed charge of the government. For two and a half months it acted as deputy for the monarchy. It gave a definite form to the constitution. On September 3, 1791, the wording was completed. On the fourteenth, Louis XVI, his powers as constitutional sovereign restored, took a solemn oath before the Assembly swearing fealty to the constitution. It was the last hope of carrying out the Revolution with the consent of the

59

monarchy. On October 1, the Legislative Assembly succeeded the Constituent Assembly, which, having completed its mission, disbanded.

The first assembly of the Revolution was certainly its most distinguished, for it represented the elite of France and accomplished great things. It swept away the Old Regime with unparalleled speed and traced in broad outline a new order, boldly and with breadth of vision. In 1790, it drafted an address to the people which gave an exact and moving account of its work. Its author, Talleyrand, declared:

Some pretend to ignore the good that has been achieved by the National Assembly, but we are going to remind you. . . . The rights of man were unknown; slighted for centuries, they have now been reestablished for all humanity. . . . The nation had lost the right to make laws and to impose taxes: this right has now been restored. . . . Innumerable privileges, irreconcilable enemies of the public welfare, which were imbedded in the common law, are now destroyed. . . . A vexatious feudalism, so powerful in its last vestiges, and overspreading all France: it has disappeared, never to return. Long have you wanted the abolition of the sale of public offices and the fees charged by the magistrates: they have been abolished. You felt the need for reform of the principal defects of the criminal code: it has been decreed. Finally, the finances have cried out for great reforms . . . we have worked without rest, and soon you will enjoy the benefit.

What Talleyrand said was so. Unfortunately, this great work had one grave defect: it was precarious. Eight years later it would be completely obliterated by the second French Revolution, the *coup d'état* of the 18th Brumaire, and by the constitution of the year VIII.

How did this first revolution lead to the second? And how to explain that it came to life again only with the Restoration? In its weakness, the Constituent Assembly, as we have seen, made two fundamental errors that are enough to account for subsequent events. The first mistake was the Civil Constitution of the Clergy, and the second was the arrangements for the executive power.

The Civil Constitution of the Clergy had been a terrible mistake. It involved the Revolution in an unrelenting struggle with the Catholic Church, a struggle that has not ended even today and has done irreparable injury to both sides. This conflict is the basis for the most serious political and social difficulties France has faced for the past century and a half.

As for the organization of executive power, the Assembly tried to resolve the problem in three different ways which eventually canceled each other out and made chronic the anarchy that followed the taking of the Bastille.

The simplest solution would have been to restore the king to his former power. The Assembly at first, in the law of September 1789, recognized Louis XVI as the head of the executive power. When, however, it came to giving him the means to exercise it (an army and control of the police), the Assembly feared that this power would be used against it and the Revolution. It then sought an alternative solution and passed the decree of December, which assigned a great part of the executive power to the assemblies elected by the people. This system could not function in the midst of the great disorder into which France had plunged.

Self-government cannot be improvised in a few months in a country accustomed for centuries to a centralized monarchical rule. The municipalities and departmental assemblies, faced with concrete problems, did not know how to proceed. There followed a slackening in the conduct of all affairs. Since the king lacked the means of enforcement, the executive power could not function in his hands. It functioned badly and too slowly when it was handed to the people. The Assembly envisaged still another solution, the creation of committees elected by the Assembly, which would have extensive powers and which would substitute for ministers. These executive committees were at first five in number: a Committee of Investigation, really a police agency which issued writs of arrest; a Committee of Feudal Rights; a Committee on Military Affairs; a Finance Committee; and a Committee on Diplomatic Affairs.

These three organs of executive power (the king, the people, and the committees), far from coordinating their efforts, paralyzed each other. France started on an infernal circle: disorder engendered fear; fear prevented the creation of a power capable of reestablishing order; and, in the end, disorder made it impossible to put into effect the constitution of 1791. There is the point of departure of the political crisis which, thanks to the war, spread from France to all Europe.

In his work *L'Europe et la Révolution française,* Albert Sorel has written: "Political liberty was an innovation. All precedents were to the contrary. In order to make the idea a vital principle, it was necessary to throw overboard acquired ideas."

Nothing is more true. France did not yet have the elements necessary to make a representative regime function. Immediately thereafter, Sorel makes a serious mistake in alleging that the Revolution wished to overthrow the Old Regime. This is a legend which, rather than casting light on events, renders them unintelligible. The Old Regime collapsed of itself, and the Revolution was the first to be surprised. When the Estates-General met at Versailles, no one dreamed of destroying the Old Regime. They simply wanted to give France an assembly and free her from certain abuses. . . . But within six weeks the former legal structure collapsed entirely and it became necessary to put something else in its place. The destruction of the old legal structure was a historical coincidence and not the result of a preconceived plan.

Albert Sorel continues:

The anarchy arose from the same causes which made the Revolution inevitable. The triumph of sedition, the terror, the discouragement and retreat of the timid, who were the most numerous; the audacity of the turbulent, the reign of the seditious, the tyranny of the violent, who were a minority of the nation; the sudden invasion of the country by an army of the wretched and the bands of criminals who gathered as soon as the power weakened and the police slackened— these were only the symptoms of the crisis.

"Symptoms"—the word is inaccurate. This anarchy, which Albert Sorel portrays so vividly, is the effect, not the symptom, of the crisis: the result of the destruction of legality. Sorel appears to glimpse the truth in the following passage:

It is not the Revolution, properly speaking, which destroyed the government; it was because the government was destroyed that the Revolution triumphed.

This is absolutely correct. But Sorel, again oblivious of the truth of the situation, continues:

From the first assault by the mob, the agents of the state, bewildered, disoriented, without direction or support, were reduced to the role of victims or of passive witnesses of the riots of the populace. The convocation of the Estates-General was only a solemn avowal of its importance.

From the very beginning, with the first riots, the officials of the state allowed anarchy to become rampant. Sorel believes that the ancient legal system yielded to the first mob, the mob that took the Bastille. Legality was lost, however, not because of the fall of the Bastille, but because of the universal refusal to obey the law, which was the result of the fall of the Bastille. This general disobedience, unique in history, made the French Revolution possible.

64

When Sorel claims that royal authority no longer existed in 1789, his statement of fact is accurate enough. But he explains nothing when he says:

The administration vanished and the army disappeared. Nothing remained of the formidable instrument of rule forged by Richelieu and perfected by Louis XIV except an inert, soft mass that overcame those who tried to wield it.

Why had this instrument become inert? We must know. The historians of the Right attribute to the Revolution the responsibility for the fall of monarchical legality; in reality, it is the monarchy that bears the responsibility. The chief cause of its downfall was its Asiatic absolutism, a form of government alien to the traditions and spirit of Europe. It had created an instrument of power that was too frail and was disproportionate to its task. This instrument ended by being shattered.*

* Moreover, the royal family of France was aware of this responsibility. Ferrero tells of having met the Duke of Vendôme in 1906, who surprised him greatly by saying that the real responsibility for the French Revolution lay with Louis XIV. Ferrero was later to understand the profound truth of this comment, which he had first regarded as a witticism. LUC MONNIER.

CHAPTER 3
The Revolution and Europe

The Legislative Assembly was the first manifestation of a revolutionary government in France. What is meant by "revolutionary government" cannot be explained unless "legitimate government" is first defined. A legitimate government is a government in which power is granted and administered in accordance with long-established principles and rules that are agreed to by the large majority and exercised by unanimous consent, without elimination of the right of debate.

France was, in 1789, a long-established legitimate monarchy. No one contested the right of the royal family to embody the power of government. The discontent which led to the convocation of the Estates-General never ques-

66

tioned the legitimacy of the monarchical government. Neither did the National Assembly raise the question. It merely desired to enlarge the power by incorporating a representative system within the existing monarchical government.

A revolutionary government is a government in which the power is granted and administered in accordance with new, less precise, rules, which are imposed by a minority, most often by force, on the majority. The history of the French Revolution shows all the successive stages through which revolutionary governments pass before attaining final form.

The Legislative Assembly was illegitimate because it was based on principles which were still not fixed and which the majority of the French neither understood nor accepted. Popular consent did not assure the Legislative Assembly a sufficiently large base. Not being at all legitimate, it became completely and fatally revolutionary. It had been elected by a system of suffrage of two degrees. Because of indifference or lack of understanding, the large majority of the four million electors of the first degree abstained. Even if the elected representatives could be considered legitimate, they did not represent the national will, and their power proved to be weak.

The principle of legitimacy on which power rests was not understood. This was a great weakness, especially for a democratic government that required, as a necessary condition, the active participation of the people. For their part, the electors of the second degree, who belonged to the upper classes, abstained. The nobility and a large part of the richer bourgeoisie wished to have nothing to do with the Revolution. Foreseeing a catastrophe, they refused to become involved in public affairs; besides, many of the nobles had already emigrated. Finally, the practicing Catholics, for reasons stated, had not participated in the elections. These abstentions removed all traces of legitimacy from the Legislative Assembly.

On May 17, 1791, the Constituent Assembly decreed that its members were not to sit in the new assembly. Perhaps it wanted to give proof of its disinterestedness. This decision did not prove to be fortunate. That is not to say that the Legislative Assembly was composed of men without experience. The majority of them had served their apprenticeship in the departmental and municipal assemblies. The Legislative Assembly was, however, composed almost exclusively of men less than thirty years of age; sixty of its members were not yet twenty-six years old. The influx of younger people is a phenomenon that accompanies every violent break with legality. Having less experience than men of a mature age, the young have more *élan* and allow themselves to be drawn by the spirit of adventure. They are also more impressionable. They launch into great enterprises, but are alarmed when confronted by the first difficulty, and take fright and compound folly upon folly. This influx of youth led to the Consulate, that is, to the submission of France to a young man of thirty. Chance would have it that in two of the other great states of Europe, Germany and Russia, the rulers were also young. In 1792 Francis II succeeded his father as emperor at twenty-four, and in 1801 Alexander I of Russia succeeded his father, Czar Paul, at twenty-three. The policies of these young men led to the Treaty of Campoformio, which plunged Europe into a general war.

The Legislative Assembly was quite different from the Constituent Assembly. The latter had represented all classes in France. The Legislative Assembly represented only one, the bourgeoisie, and only one part of that class, those who supported the Revolution. Among the 745 deputies of the Legislative Assembly were a handful of nobles, a score of constitutional priests, and a few representatives of the rich bourgeoisie. Almost the entire membership was recruited from the middle classes and the liberal professions; four hundred were lawyers from the provinces; others were journalists, intellectuals, and little known literary figures and poets. Not one was eminent in any important branch of human activity.

On the Right there were 264 deputies belonging to the monarchist Feuillants; on the Left, only 136 deputies from the Jacobin club. In October 1791 this association was not as extremist as it was later to become. Very few Jacobin deputies, among whom one distinguishes the Girondists, were republicans. The majority remained royalist, on the condition that the monarchy would subscribe to the constitution of 1791 in the broadest democratic sense. As for the mass of representatives who wavered between the two groups, the Jacobins could not count on more than a hundred among them.

The large majority of the Legislative Assembly was

moderate and conservative. It wished to implement the constitution in the spirit of a truly representative government and to adapt the new institutions to the monarchy. How to account for the fact that less than a year later these monarchists overthrew the monarchy?

The Legislative Assembly became revolutionary by the force of circumstances. It was isolated in the country. The principle of democratic legitimacy, which should have justified its right to govern, did not do so because this principle was not recognized by the majority of the nation. What were the consequences? The Legislative Assembly was seized by fear and did not know how to apply the principles of representative government with the energy and the understanding necessary to make itself legitimate.

A representative government is a government of the majority. The Legislative Assembly could not become legitimate unless its majority exercised power. But, deprived of a solid base in the country and unsure of itself, it could not succeed. It did not know how to govern. It allowed itself to be carried away by the minority which intimidated it. The republican minority of the extreme Left, headed by men such as Marat, Danton, and Robespierre, exercised upon it a continual and decisive influence. Momentarily dispersed after the massacre of the Champ-de-Mars, the extreme Left did not delay in regrouping and profiting from the weakness of the Assembly to agitate violently against it. The extreme Left was supported by the frenetic campaigns of the press, which skillfully exploited the suffering of the people.

"You suffer, you lack bread, you have no work; it is the fault of the counterrevolution, it is the fault of the king, and the Assembly, which supports the king." The myth of the counterrevolution was exploited methodically. The upper classes *would* have made a counterrevolution in 1791 and 1792 if they could, but they lacked the means. Hence, in fact, it was against a specter that the Revolution fought.

Many Girondists were discontented with the turn of events; they feared that the Revolution was threatened by an impending catastrophe; they were obsessed with the counterrevolution. Their spiritual state was a result of their disillusionment. They felt deceived. The young generation of '89 had nursed grand illusions. They had believed that the destruction of the Old Regime would mark the beginning of a new era. But nothing was changed after the fall of the Bastille. There were still rich and poor, and those who became leaders ruled badly, and those who should obey did not. The economic crisis persisted; disorder and fear reigned. And these young men feared for the Revolution. The emigration, which had grown to vast proportions in the past two years, was for them a clear sign of the counterrevolution. They were persuaded that the émigrés were scheming for the intervention of European countries in the affairs of France. The Declaration of Pilnitz on August 27, whereby the emperor and the King of Prussia affirmed that the events in France were of great concern to all the courts of Europe, only served to increase the fears.

Yet, in October 1791, the idea of a counterrevolution

was pure fantasy. We now know that the court was powerless and that the intrigues of the émigrés bore no results. But the Girondists were not so informed as we are today. Nothing was less likely, in fact, than the intervention of the European powers. It was not an actuality, but the danger was there, at least latently. And a latent danger leaves a more vivid impression than a real one. One can defend oneself against a real danger, but not against a latent danger, since it is, obviously, unrecognizable.

On October 21, 1791, Camille Desmoulins delivered a discourse to the Jacobins which faithfully expressed the disillusionment. He concluded as follows:

It was Paris that made the Revolution, and it is reserved for Paris to undo it: as the hopes of the patriots are put off, they recognize the nature of their illusions; their ardor cools and their cause becomes weaker each day. The people have become embittered, not consoled, by the anguish of the times. The loss of their property continues to add to the resentment of all who supported the Old Regime. Their party is strengthened by the cupidity of the shopkeepers, by all the merchants who sigh for the émigrés who were their customers. To this are added the fears of the rentiers *whose fear of bankruptcy so powerfully reinforced the Revolution but who now see no tangible results and fear that preparation for war will bring bankruptcy. I understand, above all, the weariness of the National Guard of Paris. For two years I have taken care to beat the drums, day and night, to hold them as long as possible from their cash registers, their hearths, and their beds.*

In the midst of a most profound international peace, the face of the capital has continued to bristle for the past two years as if Paris were occupied by two hundred thousand Austrians. The Parisian, constantly torn from his home for patrols, for reviews, and for exercises, becomes tired of being transformed into a Prussian, and begins to prefer his home or his business to being in the National Guard. He is honestly persuaded (to soften the word) that the National Assembly will not be able to carry out its decrees without sixty battalions, and that the Revolution can succeed only after a campaign that will be more demanding than the Seven Years' War. When will this Revolution end? We were less weary during the Old Regime.

The Old Regime might eventually have earned their support had the war not erupted and lasted for twenty-two years. It was because of the war, not by its writings, that the Revolution was to affect all of Europe. During the first two years of the revolutionary regime no serious incident disturbed France's relations with other nations. However, the princes who had property in Alsace brought on the first clash. Some of the princes of southern Germany held lands in Alsace from which they collected feudal dues. When the Constituent Assembly abolished feudal rights in all French territories, the decrees were applied to these holdings. The princes protested; the revolutionary government replied that this was a matter of internal policy. The princes insisted that it was of international concern and invoked the treaties that had been violated by the decrees of the Assembly. The unilateral abolition of a treaty without previous discussion was an unfriendly act which could be regarded as a *casus belli*. In itself, such a conflict was not serious. The princes could never attack France without the support of the empire and the House of Austria. But it was, nonetheless, serious because it attacked the principle of sovereignty and manifested, for the first time, the disdain of the Revolution for the rights of man. As with all revolutionary governments, the one that had just been established in Paris had little respect for legitimacy in general, and in particular for the five points that one finds in the eighteenth-century statements of the rights of man. The Assembly abolished the rights of the German princes as if this were the most natural thing.

A second cause of conflict was the question of the émigrés. Coincidence or not, most of them were refugees in the small German states whose princes had just been despoiled. The Revolution greatly feared the émigrés. The discourse delivered on October 20, 1791, by Brissot to the Assembly was evidence of this.

Brissot was thirty-seven. He had founded the newspaper *Le Patriote français,* which became the official organ of the Girondists. Its name should be remembered. It was, in effect, the Revolution, and in particular Brissot's newspaper, which launched the term "patriot"; little used under the Old Regime, it was to take on a ridiculous import.

The Assembly discussed the decrees against the émigrés. One of the decrees was aimed at the Count of Provence, threatening him with the loss of his claim to the regency if he did not return to France. Brissot enumerated the acts that were believed to herald the coming intervention by the European powers. But in fact France had nothing to fear. Brissot's speech set off popular agitation favoring vigorous action with regard to the German princes. It was the point of departure for the change of opinion which was to lead the Revolution into war with Europe.

Five days later, on October 25, Vergniaud delivered a speech of no less importance:

As reassured as I may be as to the events that lie in the future, I feel it no less necessary for us to build a rampart and to take all the precautions which prudence dictates. The skies are still too tempestuous for anyone to relax, believing that he is entirely sheltered from the storm; no veil can mask the malice of the foreign powers; it is truly demonstrated by the chain of events that M. Brissot has so energetically brought to mind in his discourse. The outrages against the national colors and the declaration of Pilnitz are clear signs of their hatred for us, and wisdom dictates that we profit from it. Their present inactivity hides, perhaps, a deep plot. They are trying to divide us. Who knows if they seek to lull us into false security?

Let us take stern measures, let us no longer allow the seditious groups to interpret our generosity as weakness, let us impress Europe with our boldness, let us dispel the phantom of the counterrevolution around which are rallied the insane who desire it; let us rid the nation of this burden of insects thirsting for its blood and causing it disturbance and fatigue; and let us calm the people.

After making a very reassuring assessment of the situation, Vergniaud, fearing possible danger in the future, concluded that it was urgent that decisive measures be taken against the émigrés.

On October 31, the Assembly voted the decree against the Count of Provence. On the same day, Montmorin, the Minister of Foreign Affairs, tendered his resignation. The ministers found themselves in an ever more difficult situation. Since the Revolution they had had to serve two masters: the king and the Assembly, which made the laws and held the purse strings. These two masters not only were not in accord with each other, they were not even in accord among themselves. A whole month was to pass before Louis XVI was able to find a new minister of foreign affairs. His place was taken during the interim by a committee of the Assembly. It was at this time that the émigrés and the princes who offered them hospitality were discussed.

On November 8, the Assembly voted the decree against the émigrés, threatening them with the death penalty if they did not return by January 1. It also charged the committee to draw up measures that the king was to take against the states that had given the émigrés refuge. On November 22, the committee gave its report. It was on the whole moderate. No one wanted to risk anything yet.

On November 27, another young Girondist, Ruhl, intervened and resumed the arguments of Vergniaud. While declaring that the émigrés were not dangerous, he insisted on the necessity of getting rid of them. He poked fun at the small German principalities; later he attacked the empire:

76

Do not be scornful, gentlemen, of the apparent slumber of the despots around you; it is the sleep of a lion which stalks its prey and rushes upon it believing that it cannot escape his claws or his carnivorous teeth. Leopold, who has been painted to you as so peaceful, whose public statements are so inconsistent with the applause of our émigrés, but whose secret actions are not known to us, Leopold will never forgive you for having put into practice the principle that kings are made for the people and that the people are not the property of the king.

On the same day, Daverhoult presented a motion, much stronger than that proposed by the Committee on Foreign Relations, requesting the king to resort to military force if, after three weeks, the prince electors of the Rhineland had not expelled the émigrés.

The next day, on November 28, Robespierre spoke at the Jacobin club. Later he was to declare himself against the war, but now, on his return from Arras, he too succumbed to the war fever of Paris.

It is necessary to say to Leopold: You are violating the rights of man in allowing the gathering of rebels, whom we do not fear but who are an insult to our nation. We summon you to expel them without delay, or we shall declare war against you in the name of the French nation and in the name of all nations which are enemies of tyranny.

On November 29, the Committee on Foreign Relations adopted the motion of Daverhoult. The situation became increasingly more strained. On the same day, Delessart, who was Minister of the Interior, assumed the ministry of foreign affairs. He was a moderate. The atmosphere immediately became calmer. At last, foreign relations would be handled by a minister of the king and not just a committee that the foreign powers did not take seriously. But, on December 2, there was a new ministerial crisis and Narbonne succeeded to the ministry of war. Narbonne was to bring the court and the king, who until now had been merely spectators to the agitation of the Assembly and the revolutionary forces, to take extreme measures. The day that Louis XVI assumed a warlike attitude in the hope of consolidating his power, war became inevitable.

The arrival of Narbonne on the scene had immediate consequences. One week later, Louis XVI went before the Assembly to read an ultimatum addressed to the Archbishop of Trèves, requesting him to expel the émigrés. The war, which had been only a revolutionary tactic of the Girondists, suddenly became the policy of the court.

When a state is threatened, good sense demands that it put its military organization in order and that it abstain from any measure that might turn a potential danger of war into an actuality. The Revolution pursued a diametrically opposite policy. Instead of reorganizing the army, a step that was long overdue, it did all it could to create an irreparable situation by its agitation, its threats, and its obsession with counterrevolution.

Why such an absurd attitude? The men in government were not, after all, fools. The reason lies in the fact that revolutionary states cannot act otherwise. A legitimate government can have a reasonable policy because it knows what its aims are and how they can be achieved. A revolutionary government is dominated by uncertainty and fear. In this unhappy situation, war appears to be an outlet for the general disorder, a means of escaping the chaos. That is what stands out in the letters of Marie-Antoinette. She hoped that the threat of war would permit the king to reassert his power. The Girondists adopted the same reasoning. They regarded the Assembly as incapable of governing, and they hoped that the war would reinforce their power. Both were deluding themselves. The reins of authority were gone and no one could seize them. It was necessary first to fashion them once again.

On December 14, Narbonne frankly confessed to the Assembly that he hoped that the war would facilitate the reorganization of the government. "If the deadly cry of war is heard, it will be for us at any rate the signal of the great desire for order and justice. . . ."

On December 15, Brissot wrote in his journal:

War! War! That is the cry of all patriots; such is the vow of all friends of liberty spread abroad over the surface of Europe, those who can no longer await for this joyous diversion in order to attack and overthrow their tyrants. It is this war of atonement which is going to renew the face of the world and plant the banner of liberty on the palaces of kings, on the seraglios of sultans, on the chateaux of petty feudal tyrants, on the temples of the Popes and muftis. It is a holy war to which Anacharsis Cloots has just invited the National Assembly in the name of the human race.

79

Now that the king had rallied to its cause, the war party felt sure of success, and the conflict became inevitable. Brissot immediately took advantage of the situation and widened his scheme. At first he had only spoken of a defensive war against the émigrés and the princes who sheltered them. Now he became more aggressive and attacked everyone. This was a consequence, once again, of fear. We must distinguish between two types of fear: defensive fear, which leads to flight; and aggressive fear, which leads to attack. This law applies to the affairs of civilized states as much as it applies to the animal world.

The bellicosity, fanned by the Girondists, increased. But the opposition to war also increased. After the declaration of the king, the extremists of the Left, with Robespierre and Marat at their head, became pacifists. They declared that the war would bring the ruin of the Revolution and the triumph of the counterrevolution.

The situation might be summarized as follows: the Girondists and the court were in agreement about waging war, while the extreme Left, the Jacobins, and, on the right, the Feuillants, were inclined to a more moderate policy. At the end of December the conservative majority drew up a memorandum to the emperor, hoping to convince him that peace was as much in the interest of the empire as in the interest of France. The fears expressed were more than justified.

If war takes place, it will be terrible. It will be conducted in a most cruel manner. Enraged incendiaries will have the upper hand, and their counsel will prevail. The King, faced with the necessity of fighting his brother-in-law and ally, will be under suspicion and, in order not to increase that suspicion, will be obliged to use greater force and exaggerate his intentions. He will not be able to be moderate or prudent without seeming to be in league with the Emperor, thus furnishing powerful weapons to his enemies and even arousing honest men, who are always easy to delude. The émigrés, counting on the support of the Emperor, will become more obstinate, more difficult to hold in check. The quarrel will become a struggle between two extremes, and the interests of rational, sensible people, as well as the principles of humanity, will be forgotten.

The Feuillants entrusted the queen to transmit this memorandum to the Emperor. Marie-Antoinette dared not refuse, but she took care to advise her brother that peace was not, in her opinion, in the interest of the court and of France.

While these events were taking place in France, how did the court in Vienna react? On December 31, 1791, Delessart transmitted to the Assembly a note delivered on December 21 by Kaunitz, chancellor to the Emperor, to the French ambassador in Vienna. In it he declared that the Elector of Trèves had taken all desired measures to give satisfaction to France, but that he feared an attack. Kaunitz added:

The Emperor is perfectly tranquil concerning the just and moderate intentions of the most Christian King, and no less convinced of the great interest of the French government not to provoke the foreign sovereign princes by means of actions against them, but daily events are not at all reassuring as to the stability and the preponderance of moderate principles in France, or the effectiveness of the central power. Above all, the powers of the provinces and the municipalities are such as to lead to apprehension that certain actions are taken despite the intentions of the King and despite the danger of the consequences.

The serious tone of this note was obvious. It meant that the Old Regime, suspicious of the Revolution, rejected the possibility of a lasting peace. Kaunitz sensed in the Revolution the existence of new forces, indefinable and incalculable, difficult to hold back, which rendered them even more formidable. The chancellor then spoke of defensive measures taken by the Emperor on behalf of the Elector of Trèves. Narbonne having sent three armies to the frontier, Austria for her part took measures which she called defensive. Such measures are always of a defensive character for those who take them, though they may appear threatening and aggressive to others. A fatal equivocation by which war has never been prevented! The note concluded:

The Emperor is too sincerely attached to his most Christian Majesty and too concerned with the well-being of France and with a general peace not to desire keenly the removal of this serious condition which otherwise will inevitably result in the head of the states of the German Empire and the other sovereigns uniting together to maintain public tranquillity and the honor and safety of rulers. In order to effect this, the

Chancellor is instructed to open frank discussions with the Ambassador from France.

The court of Vienna envisaged a European congress to settle affairs in France ("the other sovereigns uniting together"). This was a very vague scheme, but one which Paris grasped at. If the king and queen, as evidenced by their correspondence, expected much from the congress, it became the *bête noire* of the revolutionaries.

The note of Prince Kaunitz produced a sharp impression on the war party and gave substance to the specter of the counterrevolution. On January 17, Brissot violently attacked the Emperor. Vergniaud did the same. On January 25, this bellicose agitation brought on the passage of a decree which became the reply of the Assembly to the note of Prince Kaunitz:

1. The King is called upon to declare by a message to the Emperor that henceforth he will not deal with any power except in the name of the French nation and by virtue of the powers delegated to him by the Constitution.

2. The King is called upon to ask the Emperor if, as head of the House of Austria, he intends to live in peace and in mutual understanding with the French nation and if he renounces all treaties and conventions directed against the sovereignty, independence, and security of the Nation.

3. The King is called upon to declare to the Emperor that if he fails to give to the Nation, before March 1, full satisfaction concerning the points listed above, his silence, as well as any evasive and dilatory response, will be regarded as a declaration of war.

4. The King is called upon to continue to take the most prompt measures in order that the French troops be in a state of readiness to enter on a campaign when the first orders are given them.

In communicating this ultimatum to Austria, Delessart, who wanted peace, added a memorandum in which he endeavored to tone down the aggressive character of the note. After reading it to the Assembly, he added:

In conclusion, gentlemen, I express to you in one word the wish of the King, of the Council and, I do not fear to say, of the sane part of the nation: it is peace that we want. We ask a cessation of this costly state of war to which the force of events has dragged us; we want a return to the state of peace. But we have many good reasons for being uneasy and we must be fully reassured.

Kaunitz replied with a very harsh note:

As for the internal condition of France, instead of inviting us to share in the favorable augury of M. Delessart as to the return of order, the authority of government, and the exercise of the laws, France manifests, on the contrary, daily symptoms of growing inconsistency and disquiet. The powers friendly to France have good reason to fear that the King and the royal family will suffer from the same excesses which they have experienced more than once and that France will plunge again into one of the greatest evils that can afflict a great state, popular anarchy.

Kaunitz touched the Revolution at its vital nerve. What he said was true. France was in such a state that the other nations were not able to enter into normal relations with her. As Kaunitz said:

This is also a most contagious evil for other peoples; more than one foreign nation has provided the most terrible examples of its spread. It is necessary to allow other powers the same right to maintain their constitutions that France claims for herself. There is nothing more legitimate, more urgent, and more essential than the pacification of Europe.

This was very true. The anarchy in which France found itself concerned all Europe. Kaunitz further insisted that it was the Girondists, not the émigrés, who were responsible for the ferment in France—which was also true.

Prince Kaunitz's note was read to the Assembly on March 1. But during the preceding night an event had taken place which the Legislative Assembly was only informed of a week later: the death of the Emperor Leopold at the age of fifty-two. His son, Francis II, became head of the House of Austria at the age of twenty-four. Far from remaining in the shadows, he became one of the leading personalities of his time. During the first fifteen years of his reign he committed several serious errors. The greatest of these was the Treaty of Campoformio, which marked the beginning of great disorder in the West. Later, having learned his métier, he endeavored to make amends.

Francis's views were quite different from those of his father. Leopold had been sympathetic to the Revolution when it attempted to assure the state a larger and more popular base. No doubt, a revolution that destroyed the established institutions was alarming. Yet, for all that, Leopold did not fail to admire the new ideas. Francis II, on the contrary, had not differentiated between the two revolutions; he was as hostile to the one as to the other.

Leopold was German by education and in his leanings and temperament. Francis II was wholly Italian, born and brought up in Florence. His father had been the Grand Duke of Tuscany before becoming emperor. Francis II was not prepared for the office he was to assume. He was brought up in the spirit of old Italy, the Italy that had fashioned the Counter Reformation, that somber totalitarian regime imposed by the papacy, which was very much opposed to the new ideas of the Revolution. He had scarcely mounted the throne when he began to attack the Revolution. This was a grave embarrassment for the French government, but there were compensations. The emperor, so young and so little German, did not have much chance of exercising any great influence in Germany. This circumstance would be useful in Paris, where the war party showed itself of two minds. The king and the court only wanted to undertake the semblance of a war against the House of Austria, a brief and limited war that would end in the convocation of a European congress. They sought to go to war against the empire without permanently severing their alliance with Austria. The Girondists and Narbonne intended, on the other hand, to engage Austria to the limit and, while safeguarding the empire, to reverse the alliances. They sought to sever Prussia from Austria, and the negotiations were primed for that end. Narbonne had himself tried to get the Duke of Brunswick, a liberal prince, head of the Freemasons, and one of Frederick II's ablest lieutenants, to come and organize the French army, becoming its commander-in-chief. Brunswick had politely declined, but he was undoubtedly flattered by the offer.

When on March 1 Delessart read to the Assembly the note that he had sent to Austria, and its response, news of the death of Leopold had not yet reached Paris. Lively discussion ensued when the contents of these notes became known. The Girondists attacked Delessart's note for its criminal weakness, and the minister was accused of having betrayed the interests of France. The Committee on Foreign Affairs was called upon to conduct an inquiry into his conduct and to report to the Assembly. They began their work immediately, and Brissot, head of the war party, was named secretary.

On March 9, Leopold's death finally became known in Paris. The prevailing impression was that the position of Austria was weakened and that France would profit by adopting a more vigorous posture. Poor Delessart suffered the consequence. Brissot demanded his resignation and accused him of high treason. At the same time, Brissot demanded that the empire renounce all thoughts of a congress. This congress had never been more than a vague and distant project, but the ultimatum obliged the court at Vienna not to abandon it. It was a matter of prestige.

The Assembly approved both of Brissot's propositions. The mobs which invaded the tribunes and applauded the partisans of war kept the other speakers from being heard.

Those ministers who did not want to carry for long the responsibility for this political folly resigned. Louis XVI understood that it would not be easy for him to organize a new government. He addressed himself to the Girondists and advised them that he would select the men they recommended. By this step, the king abdicated part of his power to the Assembly. Three men were proposed to him, the best known of which, Dumouriez, was given the foreign-affairs portfolio. Dumouriez was at heart a convinced monarchist who never believed that France would carry out an experiment in parliamentary rule without the king. He wanted to reestablish monarchical authority in order to strengthen representative institutions. Dumouriez was a partisan of war. He believed that it was in the interests of France to engage the House of Austria fully. He became one of the first proponents of an alliance with Prussia. But before his death Emperor Leopold had signed, on February 7, a defensive treaty with the court of Berlin, to take effect in the event of a general war with France or with Russia over the Polish question. Indeed, on February 28 Prussia had notified the French government that any invasion of Germany would be regarded as a *casus belli*. Dumouriez nonetheless sought to sever Prussia from the empire.

On March 18, Kaunitz confirmed his earlier note and declared that it was in conformity with the views of the new head of the House of Austria. Dumouriez asked for further explanation, and Kaunitz replied that he had nothing to explain or add. On April 19, Dumouriez shocked the Assembly with news of this response and announced that an important message would be delivered by the king on the following day. On April 20, Louis XVI, in a moving speech, announced his decision to declare war on Austria.

Dumouriez had precipitated events for political reasons. In extracting a declaration of war from the Assembly, he believed he was facilitating the attack on Austria while Francis had not yet become Holy Roman Emperor; the new head of Austria did not receive the Imperial crown until July 14, 1792. But Dumouriez's hopes were dashed because Prussia honored its treaty of alliance.

How to explain such a war? According to the historians of the Left, it was the Old Regime which attacked the Revolution. This interpretation is erroneous. On the contrary, it was the Revolution which took the initiative in the war; the Old Regime, represented by Austria and Prussia, conducted itself in an uncertain and irresolute fashion. As for the historians of the Right, some argued that the war of 1792 was not a conflict between the Revolution and the Old Regime but rather the continuation of the wars of the seventeenth and eighteenth centuries, which resulted in the coalescence of the petty states of the Middle Ages into larger units. Albert Sorel goes so far as to say that Austria and Prussia attempted to divide France between themselves. Others support the view that the Revolution was involved in an ideological war, a war of propaganda. On this theme they have built a complete political theory and reached the conclusion that ideological wars have been the scourge of Western man and that it is necessary to guard against the example of the Revolution.

These theories are both false. The fundamental cause of the war is to be found in the mutual mistrust, created by events, between France and the courts of Vienna and Berlin. The revolutionary government was preoccupied with the fear it had inspired in legitimate governments. There was anxiety in Vienna and Berlin, and this anxiety was justified. As a consequence, Paris was also worried, and war broke out. It was the revolutionary situation in France which was responsible for the war. It would have been impossible for one or more revolutionary states to be formed in Europe without exploding into war with the legitimate states. In 1939 we witnessed a repetition of the events of 1792. Mistrust and fear led inevitably to ideological passions. Legitimate states which made war out of fear were then led to assert that the purpose of their undertaking was to restore the revolutionary state to the ranks of the legitimate governments. Such is the logic of war. The ideological issue is the result, and not the cause, of conflict.

The war of 1792 precipitated an internal crisis in France and led to the fall of the monarchy. According to the constitution, the king should have conducted the war.

But Louis XVI lacked soldiers, officers, ministers. From January 1 to August 1, 1792, a period of seven months, four ministers succeeded one another. The third of them resigned on June 10, in the midst of battle, and his successor was not named until June 23; for twelve days no one was found to replace him. Under these conditions it is not difficult to understand the military disasters.

In the month of May, the French army attempted to invade Belgium. Although it faced weak Austrian garrisons, the French army fell back and finally was forced to abandon all offensive moves. This defeat was immediately ascribed to treason. It was the king, the commander of the army, who was to blame. There followed violent popular demonstrations in Paris and in the countryside. The Jacobin extremists Marat, Danton, and Robespierre left no stone unturned to channel this discontent and use it for their own very precise ends.

During this time the National Assembly approved two bills. The first reinforced earlier measures taken against the non-juring clergy, and the second provided for the establishment of an army of twenty thousand volunteer national guardsmen near Paris. This military force was intended to assure order and to protect the Assembly. Since the king refused to ratify these decrees, Roland, Minister of the Interior, practically ordered him to do so. Louis XVI then dismissed the minister. This new crisis was a further incitement. On June 17, the Assembly named a commission of twelve members charged with the urgent task of drawing up plans to save the country. It was a public acknowledgment of the desperate situation France found herself in.

On June 19, Louis XVI took an official stand against the two decrees of the legislature by vetoing them. The leaders of the extreme Left summoned the people of the outskirts of Paris to a great demonstration for the next day. A memorial was read to the Assembly, proclaiming that the will of the people could not be interfered with by the will of one person. Then the demonstrators invaded the Tuileries. They marched before the king, who wore a red hat. He remained composed, however, and refused to yield. This day nothing came of it; but the visit the sovereign people had made upon the other sovereign made a tremendous impression. The prestige of the monarchy was irreparably weakened. Demonstrations against the king multiplied throughout the country. Everywhere the municipalities organized groups of young volunteers, who, despite the royal veto, left for the capital. The most famous of these were the five hundred from Marseilles. Bearing a petition demanding the abdication of the king, they arrived in Paris singing the *Marseillaise,* an anthem that thus entered the pages of history. Similar petitions cropped up on all sides. In the general effervescence two revolutionary organs were constituted in Paris which ended up overthrowing the monarchy. One was the Committee of the National Guard. The volunteers from the provinces had established a committee of forty-six who met in the middle of July to deliberate on the situation. There were also the electors of the forty-eight wards into which Paris was divided, who regarded themselves as the true representatives of the people and took it upon themselves to meet as if they were a second assembly of the Revolution and to apprise the Legislative Assembly of the decisions they had taken.

It was in the midst of this turmoil that the famous manifesto of the Duke of Brunswick became known in Paris, disclosing the Allies' plan of war. By arousing the people's ill-will against the king, it precipitated the downfall of the monarchy. The deposition of the king began to be discussed in the Assembly. Pétion, the mayor of Paris, was the first to propose it. However, the conservative majority in the Legislative Assembly hesitated and sought to gain time. Its indecision led the republican leaders to prepare to act by force. During the night of August 9 to 10, the members of the forty-eight wards chose their commissioners, who, supported by an armed mob, went to the Hôtel de Ville, suspended the council general of the Commune, and took its place. Mandat, the head of the National Guard, who was greatly devoted to the king, was called to the Hôtel de Ville, arrested, and removed from office. Then the mob, waving red flags, marched on the Tuileries.

The red flag had become the symbol of the Revolution. Hitherto it had been emblematic of a state of siege, denoting the resort to force by the authorities against the Revolution. When on July 17, 1791, the National Guard fired on the demonstrators at the Champ-de-Mars, the red flag was hissed. This time, in unfurling it, the insurgents proclaimed a state of siege against royalty.

The Tuileries were defended by nine hundred Swiss

mercenaries, two thousand national guardsmen, and two hundred men of the upper classes. Louis XVI renounced all resistance and took refuge with his family in the Assembly. The struggle nevertheless went out of control, costing the insurgents about one hundred men and raising the people to the height of fury. Louis XVI was accused of having drawn them into an ambush in order to massacre them.

After the victory of the populace, a delegation of the insurrectionary Commune presented itself before the Assembly. Ostensibly it came to discuss with the Assembly the measures to be taken for the public safety, but in reality it demanded the abolition of the monarchy. Legally, the Commune was nothing. The Legislative Assembly, as weak as it was, could claim a more rightful title to represent the nation. But it had been reduced to a small minority. Of the 750 representatives, only 284 were left. Thus, it was a wholly revolutionary power that presented itself before a power that was only semi-revolutionary. The Assembly was without means of defense, and the Commune had the advantage of being supported by the people in arms. In this critical situation, the Legislative Assembly had no choice but to bow to necessity.

It decreed the suspension of the king, named a provisional council of six ministers with executive power, and called upon the French people to elect a national convention which would assure the sovereignty of the people and the reign of liberty and equality. Every Frenchman twenty-one years old became a voter, regardless of property. It was universal suffrage in one leap: the doctrine of popular sovereignty, that is, that no government is legitimate if power is not delegated to it by the people. But who are the people? The most diverse answers to this question all lead to limiting sovereign rights to a part of the population, in general to the well-to-do and the educated. These solutions are wrong because they are illogical: "the people" can only be the sum total of the citizens. Thus, inevitably, one comes to universal suffrage, even if no one wants it. A political system, whatever it may be, responds to internal principles which in the end always impose themselves.

While it waited for the Convention to be elected, the Commune governed from the Hôtel de Ville. It zealously filled the prisons with those suspected of being counterrevolutionaries. Why? Because of fear. Revolutionary governments are always afraid, because they have gained their power by force, and force is by nature unstable and transitory. Power gained in this fashion is not based on any principle of law recognized by those who must obey.

The fact that royalty, which had seemed to be the moving force behind the counterrevolution, had been overthrown should, logically, have allayed the fear of the revolutionaries. It only served to augment it. This is an unalterable law: the more a revolutionary government defeats its adversaries, the more it is afraid. The invasion by the Austro-Prussian armies in the second fortnight of August further increased this fear. On the twentieth,

Logwy was occupied, and on the thirtieth, Verdun. In Paris the agitation became a paroxysm which culminated in the September massacres.

Danton offered the following explanations of the executions: "The Republicans are a tiny minority; the rest of the population leans toward the royalists; it is necessary to intimidate the royalists." It is always the same. A government that feels weak and is afraid brings the terror.

It was in this climate of fear that France proceeded to the election of the Convention, which met for the first time on Thursday, September 20, 1792.

CHAPTER 4
The Convention

There is no exact account of how the Convention was elected. Is this because of the confusion that was widespread during these troubled times? Or is it because the researches of the historians are incomplete? In any event, whether out of indifference or because of hostility toward the new regime, the adversaries of the Revolution did not participate in the elections. The abstentions were numerous, as had been the case in the Legislative Assembly. In certain districts, fewer than one quarter of the registered electors voted. Balloting was open. It began during the executions, while the counterrevolutionaries, real and imaginary, were being rounded up. The electoral assemblies had been purged previously. Not a single candidate of the opposition dared show himself. The members of

97

the Convention all belonged to the minority that had led the Revolution since August 10 right up to the September executions. There were also those who favored the newly established order because of their own special interests; for example, those who had purchased state securities, the value of which depended upon the success of the Revolution.

With the Convention, the right of opposition was abolished for the partisans of the Old Regime; the right of opposition remained the exclusive privilege of the adherents of the Revolution. The Convention was an assembly made up only of partisans, who, in the beginning at least, still recognized the right of discussion.

The Convention was composed almost exclusively of men from the legal profession: lawyers, notaries, former magistrates. The Constituent Assembly had represented all classes of the French nation. The Legislative Assembly had represented only one: the bourgeois intellectuals. The Convention went even beyond this; it represented not a class but a profession. Most of its members were without parliamentary experience. Of the 749 deputies, 486 had not participated in either of the two preceding assemblies.

The Convention, which was to have represented the majority of Frenchmen, represented only the minority. This must not be overlooked if its actions are to be understood. There is a contradiction between what the Convention was, in reality, and the principle of law under which it claimed power. It found itself in a difficult and dangerous situation, as does every illegitimate government which is not supported by the majority who are supposed to obey it. What made its position worse was that it was forced to take on an enormous task to which even a legitimate government of long standing would have proved unequal. This assembly, more than half of whom were novices, took the place that heretofore had been occupied by the king and the court. It was called upon to become the mainstay of the new regime. It was the Convention which had to insure order, make and execute the laws, and respond to the exigencies of administration. And in the face of such an overwhelming task, not only was the Convention unable to claim any rights under the law; it had no means of governing. It had no army, no organized administration, no money. It was faced by a grave financial crisis as a result of inflation, and by unrest caused by rising prices. And, in addition, France was at war with the two strongest military powers in Europe: Austria and Prussia. The war caused the greatest alarm. The country had been invaded and the enemy was marching toward Paris. On September 17, the French army had to abandon its line of defense at the Argonne. The rear guard, attacked by Prussian hussars, dispersed and fled back to the capital, crying treason. That this new government, unable to fall back on tradition or on legal right, floundered in the midst of the greatest difficulties and became panic-stricken is very easy to understand. The Convention was a revolutionary government overcome by fear. To understand its actions, we must start from there.

The Convention found itself faced with these alternatives: monarchy or a republic. On the one hand, there was a popular movement that sought the abolition of the monarchy; on the other, the majority of the people of France were unable to break with the regime to which they had been accustomed. The problem appeared insoluble. The republic was both impossible and necessary: necessary because one could not put Louis XVI back on the throne after having dismissed him twice. The authority of the king must be sovereign; otherwise, it is non-existent. One might consider his abdication. But who would replace him? The Dauphin was an infant; a regent would have to be found. Both of the king's brothers had emigrated, and the Duke of Orléans, head of the younger branch of the family, was about to renounce his title and call himself Citizen Equality. There was even mention of the son of the King of England, and of the head of the allied armies, the Duke of Brunswick.

The alternative was the proclamation of a republic. Without any preparation, and just at the moment when France was being invaded, how could a republic be organized? Where would the authority be found to establish it? To proclaim a republic would be suicide. Nonetheless, the decision was made. On September 21, the Convention voted to do away with royalty. The decree was passed by unanimous vote of the deputies present, 371 out of 749. On the following day another decree specified that henceforth public acts would be dated from the year I of the Republic.

The Republic was voted by a minority of the Convention, which in turn represented a minority of France. This proclamation was not a premeditated act, nor was it the result of long preparations; it was an incident, but an incident of gigantic proportions. No one had thought, in 1789, of establishing a republic in France. The only republics that existed in Europe at that time were oligarchies such as Venice and Genoa. The Revolution could not take them as models. What the revolutionaries wished to establish in France had to be based on an elective principle and not on heredity. No such system was known in Europe. There was only the United States of America, which in 1776 had constituted itself as a democratic republic. But the United States was far away and its institutions were new.

In America, the republican experiment had fewer obstacles to overcome than had France, a country more aristocratic even than England, where most of the privileges were reserved to the eldest son. There were scarcely any noble families in the English American colonies, and the authority of the king made itself felt only from afar. The population was Calvinist, that is, republican and democratic in its tendencies. The idea of founding a government without a king and without a nobility right in the middle of Europe was a great novelty, an adventure so extraordinary that no one could believe in its permanence. How was it arrived at? The revolutionaries began by dethroning the king. That was tackling the problem from a negative standpoint. But at a given moment the monarchy collapsed and it was impossible to restore it, the

Dauphin being a minor and the king's two brothers being in exile. The American expedient was grasped out of desperation, to escape from a predicament that had no solution.

A kind of miracle occurred which completely changed the course of events. On October 1, the Prussian army, which had stopped its advance several days earlier, began to retreat and took with it the Austrian army. On October 12, Verdun was evacuated; on the twenty-third, the enemy went back across the frontier. The danger of invasion, for the moment at least, had been turned aside. The new republic had repulsed the aggression of the two greatest military powers in Europe, whose armies one had fully expected to see entering Paris.

How did this miracle happen? The traditional explanation, and the explanation of the historians, whether of the Left or of the Right, is Valmy: the Battle of Valmy on September 21, which had repulsed the invasion. But no battle had been fought, as we know.

After a series of complicated maneuvers based on eighteenth-century strategy—seeking to economize with human lives as much as possible because the recruitment of armies was difficult—the Prussians and the French both found themselves in a paradoxical situation. The French army turned its back on the frontier and blocked communications between Germany and the Prussians, and the Prussians did the same between Paris and the French. The Duke of Brunswick, wishing to extricate himself from this situation, on September 20 moved his troops through a dense fog. The rear guard of the Prussians was about to clash with the advance guard of the French. Several cannon volleys were exchanged. Toward noon the fog cleared, and the French awaited an attack. But the Prussians broke off the battle and retired. That was the Battle of Valmy, which cost the Prussians only two hundred men and the French only three hundred.

There was nothing strange about the Prussian army retiring. This often happened during wars in the eighteenth century. The retreat merely signified that the Prussians preferred to wait for another occasion to give battle. No one would ever have spoken of Valmy if eight days later the Prussians had not been defeated while in retreat. It is not difficult to establish the cause and effect relationship with regard to the Prussian retreat at Valmy. The Revolution ascribed it to necessity: the French had driven back the Prussians. In reality, the retreat was due to other causes, the principal one being the invasion of Poland by Catherine II of Russia. It was Poland that made the Prussians hesitate and then break off the battle and evacuate France.

It is necessary, also, to take into account the insurrection of August 10. There was a tacit understanding between the invading army and the court of France. The fall of the monarchy forced Prussia into a great dilemma. What should she do if her armies entered Paris? To which government should she look for support? Moreover, the military effectiveness of France, far from being diminished by the Revolution, had increased. Many young

men enlisted enthusiastically; many also because of unemployment. France had a numerical superiority over the
monarchies of the Old Regime, who recruited their
soldiers with great difficulty.

There were several considerations which led Prussia
to turn back to its initial project: to combat the Revolution,
but in concert with all the European powers. Prussia informed Austria that she would not pursue the struggle
unless all the states of the empire cooperated to the
measure of their means. If she could count only on the
support of Austria, Prussia would seek compensation in
Poland. In fact, Prussia threatened to conclude a separate
peace with France. What happened after Valmy was the
consequence not of defeat but of the vacillating policy
of Prussia. The court at Berlin found itself in a difficult
situation, as happens when a nation is brought by a skillful sovereign to assume responsibilities it cannot handle,
and then this sovereign is succeeded by one of lesser capa-
bilities.

The retreat of the Prussian army was attributed in
France to the irresistible spirit of the Revolution. The
party which thought that this spirit was a substitute for a
military organization prevailed over the conservative elements, who remained convinced that the only basis for the
military might of a state was adequate preparation. Instead of profiting from the Prussian retreat by reorganizing its army, the Convention, encouraged by its success,
had no other thought than to invade Belgium. This was
the beginning of general warfare.

The new revolutionary government consisted of civilians. It was the civilians who, for the first time, directed the conduct of the war; only civilians could have thought of taking the offensive. On September 30, Custine, whose army had penetrated into Germany, occupied Spire. On October 24, the provisional executive council decreed that the French armies were not to put down their arms until the enemies of the Republic had been driven to the other side of the Rhine. The task of invading Belgium was assigned to Dumouriez. On November 6, he defeated the Austrians at Jemappes. On the fourteenth he entered Brussels. This victory aroused the greatest enthusiasm and bolstered the myth of the power of the revolutionary armies. On November 19, this led to a decree by the Convention, passed by unanimous vote:

The National Convention declares in the name of the French nation that it accords fraternity and assistance to all people who wish to recover their liberty, and charges the executive power to order the generals to render assistance and to defend those people who are suppressed or who may suffer in the cause of liberty.

The National Convention decrees that the Executive order the generals of the French Republic to have printed and proclaim the preceding decree in various languages in all the lands in which they enter with the armies of the Republic.

Why have historians until now paid so little attention to such extravagant actions? Driving Austria and Prussia to the other side of the Rhine was nothing less than the destruction of the Holy Roman Empire, the sacking of

Germany, the reversal of the European balance of power, the provoking of a general war. If we consider the military situation of the Republic at the end of 1792, such projects appear fantastic. In this critical period of transition, the army of the king no longer existed and that of the Republic was only coming into being. The forces of France were scarcely sufficient to defend the country against a hesitant enemy and were little inclined to court the risk of invasion. Ten years would not have been too long to constitute an army capable of carrying out a political offensive on such a gigantic scale. Even if the coalition had intended to destroy France by waging a war to the death, the proclamation of the executive council was still an act of folly. But no such thought existed in Vienna or Berlin or in the rest of Europe.

Doubtless, the Revolution could not have known this. Given the uncertainty as to the plans of its adversaries, and the state of weakness and lack of preparation in which the Revolution found itself, a purely defensive policy was called for. The Convention was not an assembly of harebrains. It was composed, in the majority, of serious men, intelligent and cultivated. If most of them lacked experience in military and diplomatic affairs, a small measure of common sense would have sufficed, it would seem, to understand that France could not attack the rest of Europe without committing suicide. How could a republic, scarcely out of its swaddling clothes, take upon itself with such ease and without opposition such a bold initiative? This audacity was but a manifestation of fear. France seriously believed in a master plot hatched by all the monarchies of Europe to annihilate France and the Revolution in concert with the émigrés and the Paris court. It would not be an exaggeration to say that the Convention officially consecrated this fear into a European coalition, which had never existed except in an embryonic state destined to be aborted.

The Convention, having no basis in law, could not rule except by force. But the National Guard existed only on paper. The organization of the army had hardly begun. It could not be used in the civil war without the risk that its spirit of patriotism in the face of foreign enemies would thus be crushed. The Convention understood this and saved the Revolution. In the general anarchy the only forces the Convention could depend on were the armed bands organized by the municipality of Paris from among the workers and the petty bourgeoisie of the capital and those who throughout France submissively accepted the slogans of the Jacobins. They had been disciplined, for better or for worse, by the specter which had been raised before them, of a world-wide coalition against the Revolution. How could such a poorly equipped government as the Convention, the existence of which depended on the popular masses of Paris—and plagued by fear as well— hope to prepare a systematic defense?

Since 1791 France had been through a severe economic crisis. The circulation of assignats had caused serious inflation. In itself, the emission of paper money, backed by the church property confiscated by the state, and accepted by the state for all payments, was an ingenious idea. Carried out with prudence, it would have been of great service. If a proper ratio between the emission of paper money and the property sold had been maintained, there would have been no inflation and the funds would have returned to the state treasury to the extent that the property was bought. But the need for money increased, especially after the declaration of war. Bundles of assignats were thrown on the market; the assignats multiplied out of all proportion. Hence their value continued to drop. At the same time the consequences of another experiment were being felt, an experiment of no less importance: the abolition by the Constituent Assembly of the controlled economy of the Old Regime.

By the eighteenth century, it had been recognized that the regulation of the economy by the state ran counter to the goals it pursued. Designed to assure the economic well-being of all classes, such regulation, on the contrary, impeded production and the circulation of wealth. The Constituent Assembly abolished the restrictive economic laws and insured the broadest industrial and commercial freedom. These liberties were soon abused, however. The speculators were the ones who profited. This situation ended by alarming the masses, who thought that the rise in the cost of living was caused by economic liberty rather than by inflation. In the latter part of 1791 the Assembly found itself faced with a demand for a return to a controlled economy. The movement was strong and was united in demanding the overthrow of the monarchy. The

Assembly attempted to resist it. Disturbances ensued when the people did not obtain the measures for which they had been clamoring. Soon those disturbances completely paralyzed the trade in grains throughout two-thirds of France. Bread began to be scarce even in departments where wheat was still abundant, for landowners preferred to hide their harvest rather than sell it at a low price.

After August 10, the economic crisis could only increase the popular unrest. There was talk of an agrarian law. The production of wheat should be reserved to the state: the first affirmation of communism. The reform that was called for first was a tax on vital necessities. How could the Convention solve these difficulties? A return to the controlled economy of the Old Regime would not only disavow the principles of the Revolution; it would aggravate the evil by transforming the shortage into famine. On the other hand, as control and collectivization of the land had their partisans among that part of the population of Paris which ardently supported the Convention, could the Convention oppose such regulation? The Paris populace must be obeyed, or, rather, given a semblance of obedience, for the Assembly was little disposed to yield. The war provided it with a useful diversion. But it was not enough. The extreme Left found another diversion in the trial and sentencing of the king.

What was the basis for this trial? The precedent of Charles I naturally weighed heavily. Above all, there was the battle that had taken place on August 10 between the people of Paris and the royal guard. Louis XVI was not responsible for the killings, but the masses were convinced that he was. One party in the Convention did not hesitate to exploit the desire of the masses for vengeance. However, the majority, consisting of the Girondists, remained indecisive.

It was the Mountain which demanded that the king be tried, both to give satisfaction to the people of Paris who were in revolt and to weaken the power of the Girondists. There was a still more profound reason, which, thanks to the sincerity of Robespierre, we know. He declared on December 3 that the king must be condemned to death even if he were not guilty, because, alive, he would always be the center of intrigue against the Republic.

To institute a legal action, there must be a charge. In default of a good reason, at least the pretext of one. But what could Louis XVI be charged with? The historians of the Left justify the trial and the sentencing of the king for treason. Louis XVI had been continuously in touch with foreign courts. We have his letters and those of Marie-Antoinette, which would be sufficient today to condemn him. However, we must remember that under the Old Regime the sovereigns of nations at war never ceased to communicate with each other. It would be a political anachronism to charge Louis XVI with high treason because of this. Since this complaint could not suffice, the Convention satisfied itself by accusing him of conspiracy against the liberty of the nation and of crimes against the general security of the state; vague and general charges which are found in all the judicial prosecutions of revolutionary governments. The guilt of the king was not even discussed, as if all the world had admitted it a priori. This is understandable if one thinks of the anger of the people and their power to intimidate the Assembly. No one dared protest against the lack of a serious basis for the charges.

The trial began on December 11 and lasted through January 19. The Mountain demanded the death penalty. The Girondists, while not openly defending the king, sought to save him by appealing to the people. They asked that the judgment should be submitted to the ratification of primary assemblies. The debate was long drawn out, but the motion was finally rejected. The people would probably have saved the king. But would it have been possible to have a free vote?

On January 14, the Convention reached an agreement to put the following three questions:

1. Is Louis Capet guilty of conspiracy against the liberty of the nation and of crimes against the general safety of the State?

2. Shall the judgment be submitted to the ratification of the people?

3. What shall be the penalty?

The roll call of the Convention began on the fifteenth. Out of 721 present, 693 declared Louis guilty. On the second question, a vote by the people, the Convention was divided, 423 against 292. The third question was the most critical. After two ballots, the death penalty was finally voted, on January 18: 387 against 334. And on the twenty-first, Louis XVI was executed.

This was a great mistake. Newborn, the young Republic feared the court that it replaced. It was afraid because it was a phenomenon without precedent in the history of France and Europe. France sought to guarantee her security by exterminating the dynasty.

What judgment should posterity hand down on Louis XVI? The historians of the Left accuse him of treason; those of the Right, of weakness. But can he be reproached for not doing what he could not do? After the fall of the Bastille, Louis XVI no longer had any power. His means of acting, if not nil, were very limited. And one cannot demand of a hereditary monarch the genius that would have been necessary to face such a difficult situation. If Louis XVI was not the martyr of the Revolution, he was certainly its victim; an illustrious victim who knew how to maintain his royal bearing even in misfortune. As for his faults, they were small in comparison with those of his ancestors. They were the ones responsible for his impossible situation.

The immediate effect of the trial of the king was an increase in the popular unrest caused by the shortages and the rise in the cost of living. On January 14, the forty-eight districts of Paris had asked the Convention to fix the rates of the assignats and to abrogate the decree of May 17, 1791, which authorized their sale or exchange for gold or silver currency. Inflation had led to the circulation of two currencies: one real, of gold or silver; the other unreal, of paper, which had led to the rise in prices. The flight of gold was an organic phenomenon of the Revolution, which was, after all, a subversion of legality. For it is the rules and principles that constitute the legal basis of a civilized country which give money its chief characteristic, stability. These laws are not gratuitous. Their observance requires wisdom and honesty. Revolutionary governments are always tempted to exempt themselves from these laws by coining additional money. The immediate advantage which they gain never fails to be cancelled out later, because the false money eventually loses all value. Either it is taken out of circulation, or one must endeavor to impose it as if it had real value. The Revolution chose the second course.

The Convention having evaded the demands of the Paris districts, they again made their charges on February 3, two weeks after the death of the king:

Citizens, once again we call your attention to the decree of the Constituent Assembly declaring coined silver a commodity. This anti-civic measure which gives rise to speculation and cheating enters perfectly into the calculations of the enemies of the public good. This decree is the principal vehicle for the machinations of the enemies of liberty to overthrow the sacred edifice of our rights. . . . It is this immoral decree which gives birth to the evils with which we are at present afflicted. . . . The storm rumbles from the distance and is ready to burst over our heads. Legislators, have courage! We are stirred; speak, and the tyrants will disappear. . . . Abrogate this law, the product of incompetence and unskill-

fulness, reject a repressive decree, pronounce the death penalty on all those who, in exchanging their gold, silver, or copper for the national assignats, give less value than the law prescribes.

Once again the Convention sought to put off the question. It posed a far more serious problem for the Mountain for this popular movement to be outside its control, embodied in an extremist party which wished to profit from the death of the king and from the support of the lower classes in Paris to force the Convention into new economic legislation. This party was the Enragés; one of its leaders, Jacques Roux, demanded the death penalty for monopolists and all enemies of the Revolution. He was a forerunner of the Terror.

The trial and sentencing of the king had another consequence: it precipitated the break with England. Legend has portrayed the struggle between France and Europe as a duel between the Revolution and the Old Regime. In reality, the great absolutist courts came to terms with the Revolution and even concluded alliances with it. However, with England the war never ceased. It lasted without interruption for twenty-one years, except for a one-year truce following the signing of the peace of Amiens. This fact is all the more strange because close affinities existed between the institutions of England and those of revolutionary France. Had not France proposed to adopt a mode of government analogous to the one England had had for centuries? The primary cause of this apparent paradox was that the two countries chose different paths to achieve the same goal.

At first England had been an absolute monarchy. Following Magna Carta and other laws and agreements, the crown had recognized certain rights of its subjects. Thus was representative government born. But these laws had no other guarantee than the sanctity of contract. The contractual principle, the basis of English liberties, was not valid unless it implied the legitimacy of the authority of the king. Hence the English form of government presupposed the legitimacy of monarchical power.

At first France hoped to follow the same path. Mirabeau had proposed it in his famous speech of June 15, 1789. "You desire legislative power," he declared to the Third Estate, "and you are right. But take care not to seize it from the king by a revolutionary act. Wait until it is conceded to you; if not, you will destroy both the authority of the king and your own, which is dependent on it. You will then have no choice but to proclaim the expression of the popular will, though this will is wavering and uncertain." Mirabeau wanted to make the Third Estate understand that political evolution in France must follow the same course as in England and depend on the concessions of royal authority. However, events did not permit such an evolution to take place. Louis XVI at first sought to resist, and when he conceded it was too late. The fall of the Bastille deprived him of any means of action. Political evolution in France took on a revolutionary character, and the Assembly was forced to make use of the principle of popular sovereignty.

The doctrine of popular sovereignty, which emerged from the great political and legal strides made at the beginning of the seventeenth century, as well as from Grotius's natural law, was not new. It is founded on the idea of the equality of men, who are born with both the right to govern and the duty to obey. It is immanent in the history of mankind and reemerges each time a civilization decays.

The English system is empirical. It rests on tradition and not upon any general principle, except perhaps the sanctity of contract. It was constructed slowly, progressively, by superimposing charters on laws; by royal concessions which established little by little the mutual rights of crown and parliament. This culminated in the creation of a representative power, a parliament partly hereditary and partly representative, with a limited suffrage, haphazardly organized and facilitating corruption. In France, where the new government had no tradition on which to stand, the government was obliged to resort to philosophical doctrine.

The advantage of the English system over the French was its greater stability. In England the change was accomplished without the overthrow of the preceding regime, by adapting to the hereditary principle. There was no struggle, no break with legality, and this facilitated the functioning of the new institutions. The English system has the disadvantage of being inconsistent, however. It is not based upon clearly enunciated principles. Can Parliament, which is elected by a limited electorate, claim that it represents the English people? This empirical regime, whose mechanism of operation is difficult to explain, and which excludes a large part of the population from power, invited discontent.

The French system had other defects and other advantages. It was consistent, but the philosophical principle upon which it was based did not encompass the masses. The doctrine of natural rights and the equality of men would inevitably lead to the negation of all hereditary forms of power, and even to the negation of property itself, that is, to communism. Fénelon had recognized the dangers of this doctrine if it were carried to an extreme.

It is understandable, then, why the French Revolution aroused greater fear in England than in Russia, Prussia, or Austria. These three powers had no fear of contagion. Their workers and peasants were in no condition to revolt; they did not even contemplate it. But in England, where opinions could be voiced, the discontented greeted the French Revolution with sympathy because it pointed to a remedy against the abuses of the party in power.

This sympathy alarmed those who benefited from the English system of government, the court and the parties in power. It brought on a reaction, the most significant manifestation of which was the publication in 1790 of Edmund Burke's *Reflections on the Revolution in France*. Burke, who belonged to the Whig party and was one of the most prominent members of Parliament, indicted the principles and philosophy of the French Revolution, as against which he urged the inconsistent empiricism of the English Revolution, which he praised. England must preserve her hereditary institutions, the basis of her liberties, and reject the doctrine of natural rights. Representative institutions can never function if one obstinately persists in giving them a philosophical basis. Only terrible disorders will result, and they will give birth to governments more tyrannical than the old monarchy.

The work was an immense success. It gave expression to the fear that the revolutionary movement in France had inspired among the intellectual and political elite in England, and the hostility that the Revolution encountered at the start from parliamentary forces. This mistrust was further increased by the events of 1792: the declaration of war in April; the events of August 10 that led to an official breaking off of diplomatic relations between the two countries; and, above all, the invasion of Belgium. Though it would be an exaggeration to claim that for England Belgium was a life-or-death issue, nevertheless England was alarmed to see Belgium invaded by the French army, and even more alarmed by a decree of the Convention, on November 16, which reestablished freedom of navigation in the Scheldt in derogation of the Treaty of Westphalia. Such a measure would injure the economic interests of Holland, who complained, as did England, her ally.

"England will never consent," declared Lord Grenville, "to the powers that France has arrogated to herself to annul according to her good pleasure, under the pretext of natural rights of which she is the sole judge, the political system of Europe."

The decree of November 19, offering aid and assistance

to insurgent peoples, raised new apprehensions. Such was the English frame of mind when the execution of Louis XVI became known. It aroused a strong sentiment of reprobation in this parliamentary milieu. The English government had to make some protest. It requested that the French representative, Chauvelin, leave Britain within a week. The government hoped that this measure would satisfy public opinion without incurring the risk of war, Chauvelin not having the rank of ambassador. It was wrong. Revolutionary states are very sensitive. The Convention regarded the recall of its representative as a mortal offense and declared war on England.

At that time France had a population of nearly twenty-five million, and England had only ten million inhabitants. England possessed a not inconsiderable army and a great navy, but they were hardly superior to France's. It was the Revolution which undermined this balance of forces and assured Great Britain of supremacy on the seas. England was the richest European power in gold and silver; thanks to her commerce, she had amassed considerable stocks.

It would seem more logical for England, richer and better organized than France, to have taken the initiative for war. But England was deeply attached to the cause of peace, and it was France that seized the initiative, just as she had done a year earlier against Austria. This can be explained by psychological reasons peculiar to revolutionary governments, which are mistrustful of their subjects, for the majority disputes their right to rule. Fear is for them a means to establish their ascendency, and they use it often. Since it is easier always to take strong and ruthless measures in time of war, the danger of war is less frightening to a revolutionary government than to a legitimate one, for, whatever the outcome, war offers a revolutionary government an immediate advantage: it can impose its power more easily in wartime. Maistre aptly remarked that the Revolution was saved by the war. It was, in effect, the permanent state of war from 1792 to 1814 which permitted the Revolution to maintain and to extend in power.

The special circumstances the Revolution found itself in were to give a new character to the war, a spectacular character that was already evident in 1793. During the sessions of February 20 and 22, 1793, the Convention decreed a levy of 300,000 men to complete the republican army. Citizens from the ages of eighteen to forty, bachelors, and widowers without children, all were subject to the call. Every department was required to furnish a certain number of men. The quota could be filled by voluntary enlistments; if these proved insufficient, the communes were authorized to resort to a draft.

This decree was the origin of a military transformation that was to result several years later in conscription. War was no longer considered the specialty of a professional minority; service in the army was a civic duty incumbent upon all citizens. This idea was new in Europe, where there were still only mercenary armies. Of all the transformations effected by the Revolution, in France particularly, this had the gravest social consequences. France imposed it on the nations in the Continent with which she engaged in war. Later it was adopted by Japan, China, and by England, and finally by the United States. Until then, the Anglo-Saxon world had escaped this consequence of the Revolution.

The aim of this decree was to expand the French army. However, at the beginning of 1793 the Republic had no need of such a large number of soldiers. What was lacking was not men but staff officers. The royal army had suffered a complete disruption with the emigration of the nobles, and a new corps of officers had not yet been formed. Such a rapid increase in the number of men only aggravated the difficulties of reorganizing the army. There was no need to enlist 300,000 men. Why then this decree? It was a dramatic measure intended to impress Europe and to intimidate those who might have thought of rebelling. It was a bluff.

This *levée en masse* was not conscription. It was based on the old system, which depended on volunteers. Under the Old Regime, the armies consisted of mercenaries, foreigners most often, who were hired for a fixed period of not less than ten years. Alongside this army of professionals there existed another institution, the militia. In cases of extreme danger, the authorities could call upon all men capable of carrying arms to serve. They did not receive any military instruction and were generally used in the defense of besieged cities or in the protection of the coasts. This was not conscription, which calls all men to the colors, whether in peace or war.

During the wars of the League of Augsburg and the

Spanish Succession, the government of Louis XIV had abused the militia by employing them as auxiliary corps. This led to widespread discontent, because, though these soldiers were not paid, the generals often sent them to the most exposed battle fronts. Marshal Saxe had protested against these operations. During the eighteenth century, scant use was made of the militia, and many of the *Cahiers* sent to Versailles in 1789 demanded that it be done away with entirely. The Revolution returned to this old system, however, making frequent use of the militia, and this led directly to conscription.

The French armies were successful in Belgium. Belgium was a Catholic country that clung to the liberal traditions of the Old Regime and whose communal life was still very active. The reforms introduced by Joseph II, which violated the ancient charters, centralized the government, and destroyed the religious organizations, had aroused wide discontent. The geographical position of Belgium, which lacked a common frontier with the hereditary states of Austria, favored political separatism. Accordingly, the French armies of Dumouriez were received with sympathy. The Belgians wanted an independent oligarchy, a republic modeled after Venice, and Dumouriez had encouraged these aspirations. Since his victories had assured him of great prestige, he proposed to make Belgium the base of his operations and march into Paris, dissolve the Convention, reestablish the royal regime in the person of the young Louis XVII, who was imprisoned in the Temple, and take upon himself the regency during Louis XVII's minority. He would thus restore a constitutional monarchy.

The historians of the Left have denounced Dumouriez's project as heinous treason; those of the Right regard him as an ambitious intriguer. In fact, the project was not altogether devoid of good sense. The republic not being viable, it was necessary to return to the monarchy. But the hour of restoration had not yet come. Twenty troubled years had to pass before it did come in 1814.

Dumouriez's plan ran afoul of an unexpected obstacle. On December 15, 1792, Cambon delivered a speech, which became famous, to the Convention. The speech dealt with the revolutionary conquests.

Dumouriez, on entering Belgium, proclaimed grand principles, but he limited himself to making speeches. Until now he has spared nobles, privileges, corvées, the feudal system, etc. The old system remains. We have promised to make the people happy, to deliver them from their oppressors, but we limit ourselves to words only. The people, enslaved by an aristocracy of the clergy and the nobility, do not, alone, have the strength to break their chains, and we have done nothing to aid in their liberation.

Cambon concluded that it was necessary to use the resources of the conquered countries to prosecute the war. However, by the eighteenth century the barbaric custom of having armies live off the occupied lands had been completely abandoned. Food depots had been organized —real progress in the humanization of war.

Cambon's speech made a strong impression and led to the adoption of the following proclamation:

ARTICLE 1. *In all the countries that are occupied or will be occupied by the armies of the French Republic, the generals*

*are to proclaim, in the name of the French nation, the aboli-
tion of imposts or existing contributions, tithes, feudal dues,
personal servitude, exclusive hunting rights, the rank of nobility, and, in general, all privileges. They will announce to
the people that they bring peace, help fraternity, liberty, and
equality.*

ARTICLE 2. *They will proclaim the sovereignty of the people and the abolition of all existing authorities and that, sub-
sequently, primary or communal assemblies of the people will
be convoked to create and organize a provisional administration; they will publish, post, and execute, in the language or
idiom of the country in each community, the proclamation an-
nexed to the present decree.*

ARTICLE 3. *All the officers and agents of the former government, as well as those who were formerly members of the
nobility or of privileged corporations, are, for the first election
only, not to be admitted to provisional administrative or judicial positions. . . .*

ARTICLE 7. *The executive council will also choose the national commissioners who will meet to plan, with the provisional administration chosen by the people, those measures to
be taken for the common defense and for the procuring of
clothing and the necessary subsistence for the armies of the
Republic, and to pay their expenses. . . .*

ARTICLE 11. *The French nation declares that it will regard
as enemies of the people those who refuse to accept liberty
and equality; who, in renouncing them, wish to preserve,
recall, or treat with the prince or the privileged castes; who
do not agree not to sign any treaty and not to put down arms
until after the consolidation of the sovereignty and the independence of the people in the territory which the troops of the*

Republic have entered, who will adopt the principles of equality and establish a free and popular government.

It is a program of total war which is expounded in this long declaration. The historians of the Right see in it proof of the madness of the Revolution. In fact, however, this was not a fit of lunacy. Under threat, groups, like individuals, cling to illusions. The situation was grave and the Revolution sought to delude itself. The sympathetic reception by the Belgians was its only source of satisfaction, but Paris interpreted this in its own way. There occurred in Belgium, as in other parts of Europe, a quite natural phenomenon. When a revolution breaks out in one great nation, it is immediately imagined that changes will take place that will make for a better life. This results in an effervescence which manifests itself mainly in the middle and lower classes. So it was in Paris, and it led finally to the belief that all Europe was on the eve of a revolution.

There was something else. French finances were in a deplorable state. Soldiers were recruited, and there were no means of clothing them. They were supposed to live off the lands they had invaded, thus negating one of the most important advances of the eighteenth century. Since it could not be admitted that this was due to a lack of funds, the cry was raised that the people must be freed from slavery, in return for their defraying the costs of war. To apply Cambon's decree meant declaring war on the entire world. The Revolution was not long in finding this out. With only a few exceptions, the Revolution did not carry out this plan, but the decree was never repealed or officially disavowed.

When Napoleon invaded Italy in 1796, he had instructions not to engage in revolutionary activities and to respect the existing regime. Everywhere, however, he had dealings with small groups of desperate men who wished to bring about a revolution and who demanded that the decree of December 15 be carried out. France could not ignore them without the risk of depriving the armies of their sole source of support. The Revolution placed itself in a false situation indeed when it proclaimed revolutionary war but was neither able nor willing to carry it out.

In arousing the indignation of all Belgians, except for a few extremists, the decree of December 15 completely upset the political plans of Dumouriez. Not wishing to levy a regular contribution upon Belgium, he demanded money, supplies, and arms from Paris. The response was: "Obtain what you need from the land." The war with England was to complicate matters further. It brought with it war with Holland, and Dumouriez was ordered to invade. He did not conceal from the Convention the difficulties of such an undertaking. But he had to execute the order. He sent General Miranda to lay siege to Maëstricht while he himself invaded Holland from the west. Miranda, having been stopped in front of Maëstricht, had to retreat, and on March 5 the Austrians occupied Liége.

When on March 8 the Convention learned of Miranda's retreat, there were two different reactions. Robespierre demanded the purge of all suspected officers. Danton maintained, however, that the disorganization of the army was the real cause of the disaster and that a new effort should be made to send Dumouriez whatever he needed to carry on the fight. Robespierre and Danton thus took opposite points of view. Robespierre viewed the situation from the standpoint of the necessity of political revolution, while Danton looked at it exclusively from the standpoint of military considerations. Danton was obviously right. But for his views to prevail, a more resolute, more sanguine assembly would have been needed. In the state of fear in which the Convention found itself, Robespierre's opinions had much greater chance of gaining support. In fact, on the following day a deputy who was as yet unknown but who was later to achieve sinister notoriety, Carrier, proposed the creation of a revolutionary tribunal that would try traitors and counterrevolutionaries, without any right of appeal.

It was under these circumstances that the news of the capture of Liége by the Austrians spread through Paris on March 10. The agitation mounted. Robespierre denounced the apathy of the Convention and attacked the Girondists. To overcome the resistance of the assembly to economic measures that had been extolled by the Enragés, who were a source of great embarrassment to it, the Mountain took it upon itself to accuse the Girondists of betraying the Revolution and of wishing to preserve the king. Robespierre again demanded the purge of the government. Danton, inopportunely, came back to the need of terrorist measures and insisted that new armies had to be raised. This time, however, he did not content himself with asking only for military reforms; he demanded a reform in the government.

After the fall of the monarchy on August 10, the Legislative Assembly had named a committee of six ministers, with Danton among them as minister of justice. This committee remained in power in a situation that was not clearly defined. To whom was it answerable? To the Convention? The Convention was too large and had no authority over it. While waiting for the new constitution which a legislative committee was charged with drawing up, the ministers were responsible to no one. Hence the untenable situation: there was a sovereign, the Convention, but the ministers who should have been its right hand were independent of it. The military defeat was partially due to this lack of coordination. The Convention had indeed tried to remedy the situation by nominating a committee of general defense for the purpose of directing the ministers. However, this turned out to be inadequate.

On March 10, Danton asked that the ministers be placed under the authority of the Convention and that they be allowed to be chosen from among its members. (Members of the Legislative Assembly were barred from becoming ministers.) To gain agreement for his proposition, he consented to accept the revolutionary tribunal as demanded by the extremists. The Convention, under the pretext that no decision could be taken until the new constitution had been completed, refused to reform the executive power, but it did vote the creation of the revolutionary tribunal. There was to be no right of appeal from this tribunal, each of whose jurors was to pronounce his verdict publicly and viva voce. This procedure, which had been followed during the trial of the king, was most dangerous. No one dared to show clemency for fear of being considered a counterrevolutionary.

On March 14, the Convention received a letter from Dumouriez. To prevent an even greater disaster to his armies, he refused to apply the decree of December 15 to Belgium and asked the Assembly to approve his conduct, that is, to disavow its official decree. The president did not dare to make this letter public, and referred it to the Committee for General Defense. This committee attempted to negotiate and dispatched Danton and Delacroix to Dumouriez to persuade him to withdraw his letter. Dumouriez resumed military operations. He hoped for a victory, which would give him new prestige and facilitate the operation he intended to undertake. On March 16, he attacked the Austrians at Tirlemont and pushed them back; on the eighteenth he attacked them at Neerwinden but was defeated. His retreat turned into a rout, and he decided to evacuate Belgium and return to France. By this time the Belgian masses were in revolt. Dumouriez's political projects had collapsed. After the letter that he had written to the Convention, it was impossible for him to return to France. Hence he negotiated with the Austrians and agreed to abandon Belgium on the condition that the Austrians would not attack while he carried out military and political operations against Paris. Dumouriez arrested the commissioners of the Convention and prepared to march on the capital. But victory escaped him. On April 5, his officers refused to follow him. His army, persuaded by the emissaries of the Convention, did not want to become an instrument of the restoration of the monarchy. Dumouriez was reduced to going over to the enemy.

Thus the first attempt against the republican government failed. What did this prove? It proved that, as weak as it was, the Republic was nonetheless capable of maintaining itself, and the monarchy was incapable of reconquering France. This appeared to justify Robespierre's demand that the army be purged of suspect officers. Mistrust and fear grew in equal measure. Traitors were seen everywhere, and more than ever an alleged conspiracy by foreigners to deliver France to its enemies and to destroy the Revolution became the subject of denunciation.

CHAPTER 5
The Uprising
of June 2, 1793

To the loss of Belgium and the defection of Dumouriez was added the insurrection in the Vendée. The economic situation worsened and the inflation grew, for the war had forced the government to multiply the emission of assignats. The landowners refused to sell their grain for paper money. In his book, *La Vie chère sous la Terreur,* Albert Mathiez cites the reports that came from all the departments reiterating the same message: the stores are empty; bread is scarce; the masses are in turmoil, demonstrations are multiplying. "Give us a king, but more than that, give us bread," was the general cry. The commissioners of the Convention sent to the provinces to oversee the levy of 300,000 men were also charged with checking supplies. Their authority, first limited to the needs of the army, was extended to the civil population and they were given the right of requisition to "stock the markets." This was a return to the regulation of the Old Regime. This crisis in subsistence goods had no other cause but the circulation of valueless paper money. The revolutionary elements did not want to admit this; they saw in it a maneuver of the partisans of the Old Regime to starve the people and force a return to 1789. The shortage was nothing more than the counterrevolution in subsistence goods! On March 26, Jean Bon Saint-André, commissioner of the Dordogne, wrote to his colleague Barrère at the Convention:

The public interest, let us say clearly, is about to perish, and we are almost certain that only the most prompt and extraordinary remedies can save it . . . Our experience proves that the Revolution has not been completed and we must say frankly to the National Convention: You are a revolutionary assembly. . . .

The difficulties in the Vendée and the neighboring departments are no doubt disturbing, but they are really dangerous only because the sacred enthusiasm for liberty is being smothered in our hearts. Everywhere people are tired of the Revolution. The rich detest it, and the poor lack bread and have been persuaded that they should take it from us. The journalists have completely misled and perverted public opinion. The popular societies have entirely lost their vigor. These facts are distressing, without doubt, but they are true. . . .

We are using all our efforts to restore some strength to souls, but we are talking to corpses. Besides, all those whom we have hitherto called moderate, who somehow made common cause with the patriots, or somehow at least wanted a revolution of sorts, no longer want it today. They hope for regress, they wanted a counterrevolution, and by heart, intention, and will act with the aristocracy. Think of those colleagues who in truth seek the true faith, who really love the fatherland....

The poor have no bread, though there is no shortage of grain. The grain is, however, completely concealed; all the administrators whom we have seen have confirmed this. It is of the utmost necessity that we restore the poor to life if we wish them to aid in achieving the Revolution.

The revolutionary exasperation spread to the masses. The Mountain, like the Enragés, sought to turn the masses against the Girondists, who represented the conservative majority in the Convention. They saw only one way to restore the state of affairs which had been so compromised: recourse to violence. In his journal, Marat did not cease to preach the need of terror. The Revolution could be saved by cutting off heads. In fact, during the month of March, decrees tending to establish a regime based upon force multiplied both in Paris and in the provinces. Committees of action and of revolutionary surveillance were established in all the communes. They were appointed by the Jacobin clubs and were to keep suspects under surveillance; in the departments the commissioners of the Convention were authorized to arrest and deport suspects. Parliamentary immunity for the members of the Convention was suspended. An internal revolutionary army, known as the sans-culottes, was created and charged with the defense of the Assembly; and finally, the Committee of Public Safety was set up.

On April 4, the Convention named a commission, headed by Isnard and Danton, charged with solving the problem of government. It worked with dispatch, and by the sixth it had already voted the decree that established the Committee of Public Safety. This committee was to deliberate in secret. It was charged with surveilling and directing the ministers of the government. It could suspend their orders and take all measures necessary for internal and external defense. It had very broad powers, except for the treasury. For its part, the Convention arrogated to itself the right to send commissioners to the departments. This resembled the intendants of the monarchy. They would wear special uniforms and insignia. In this sense, the Revolution inherited the ways of the Old Regime. In three days the problem of government was resolved by the organization of a veritable centralized dictatorship, although the constitution of 1791 had sought to establish a decentralized, limited government. Now all controls were abolished. On April 6, the members who were to constitute the Committee of Public Safety were elected by the Convention, chosen from among the Montagnards, with Danton as the real head, even though he was called minister. On the same day the revolutionary tribunal went into action.

At once Danton inaugurated a bold political plan: he wanted to bring an end to the war. He was, by temperament, intuitive. He had favored a war to the knife, as by the decree of December 15, but subsequent events in Belgium had an effect upon him. It was an illusion to think that Europe was about to go through the same crisis as France. It was necessary to take stock. He became a partisan of peace. But to make peace was a difficult enterprise for the Revolution, which, unlike the Old Regime, lacked the necessary machinery for such negotiations. There was also the problem of maintaining internal order. If the dangers of war began to make an impression on Danton, many other revolutionaries were preoccupied with the price of peace. That, too, could present a danger. There was fear that the great European courts would require the restoration of the monarchy as a condition for peace.

Robespierre held forth on this fear. On April 13, a long discussion took place in the Convention concerning the letters exchanged between the Prince of Coburg, commander of the Austrian army, and the representatives of the Convention on mission to the Army of the North, in which the Austrian general made vague allusions to eventual negotiations. Robespierre used this as a pretext to denounce the dangers of such advances and wanted to outlaw and put to death all "cowards" who would come to terms with the enemy. Such a proposition amounted to announcing a perpetual war with Europe. Danton presented the following amendment: the death penalty for

135

those who proposed coming to terms with the enemy without recognizing the sovereignty of the French people, that is, for proposing to make peace with those powers which were demanding the restoration of the Old Regime as a condition of peace. Danton thus courageously attacked the politics of revolutionary war. His amendment was approved by the Convention, which declared itself ready to negotiate for peace if the enemy agreed not to interfere in the internal affairs of France. The decree of April 13 contradicted that of December 15, but it did not annul it. So the matter rested.

Danton's efforts on behalf of peace failed, however. Robespierre, who was hostile to them, replaced him in the Committee of Public Safety during the month of July. The question of peace or war was more important for the moment than the spiraling cost of living, which, however, provoked new troubles. The Enragés clamored for the regulation of food supplies. They denounced the monopolists and aroused the people against the Convention itself. On April 18, a general assembly of mayors and municipal officials of Paris and of the outlying communes addressed a petition to the Convention demanding an inventory of all grains and the fixing of maximum prices for wheat, since "the products of the soil, like the air, belong to all men."

From April 25 to May 4, in the midst of popular demonstrations, a lengthy debate took place in the Assembly. The Girondists led a vigorous opposition to the proposal, which could only aggravate the economic crisis. However, under the force of popular pressure, the measure was approved, despite the opposition of the majority. All producers of wheat were obliged, under penalty of confiscation, to make a declaration of their harvests. These declarations were subject to check by searches. The law also fixed the maximum prices for grain and flour in each department, according to the average price current between January 1 and May 1.

The price was not uniform throughout France. It could vary from one department to the other. As the Girondists had predicted, these measures led to disastrous results. They were reluctantly applied by the departmental authorities. Moreover, they gave rise to an unforeseen difficulty. The landowners sought to sell their wheat in the departments with the highest maximum prices. The departments with the lowest fixed prices found themselves without bread. This setback, far from discrediting the party which had carried out these economic measures, was turned against the Girondists. They were accused of not having applied the laws. The Enragés stirred up the people of Paris and, together with the Mountain, prepared an insurrection of the commune against the Girondists. This was a repetition of the uprising of August 10. The Convention tried to resist, by dissolving the Parisian authorities, but in vain. The Mountain prevented any action by the Convention that might have nipped the movement in the bud. On May 31, an armed mob was mobilized. The mob invaded the Convention and demanded the indictment of the Girondist leaders. To yield to such unreasonable demands would have been suicidal. Not having obtained what they wanted, the rioters renewed their demonstrations on June 2. The Convention attempted to resist. Hanriot, the head of the National Guard, surrounded the Convention. It finally had to surrender and voted the arrest of twenty-nine of its members.

The uprising of June 2, 1793, was an event of incalculable importance. It marked the definitive defeat for the first French Revolution: that of 1789, of the Tennis Court Oath and the Declaration of the Rights of Man, of Mirabeau and Talleyrand, who sought to give France a representative government based on political liberty.

The second revolution was about to begin. It would be the negation of the first. It was that of 1799 and of the 18th Brumaire, of the constitution of the year VIII and the Consulate, from which rose the first totalitarian government in Europe. The first revolution was born of the intellectual movement of the eighteenth century; the second was a child of the Great Fear. This dualism of revolutions still tears at the world today, after a hundred and fifty years. The struggle of today is only a continuation of it. The Anglo-Saxons are fighting for the revolution of '89, the totalitarian regimes for that of '99.

The Convention, it must be repeated, was not a legitimate power. It represented only a part of France. The supporters of the Old Regime were unable to have a part in it. They were rejected both as candidates and as electors. The Convention only represented revolutionary France. It did not concede the right of opposition either to the

Catholics or to the royalists. A representative regime based upon the principle of popular sovereignty is not legitimate if it does not respect the right of opposition of the minority. If the Convention did not possess this fundamental legitimacy, it could still lay claim to a legitimacy of a second order because it recognized the right of opposition by revolutionaries. At the outset it gave proof of political tolerance. Montagnards and Girondists were free to defend their ideas and to manifest their opposition. After June 2, however, a part of revolutionary France found itself violently deprived of this right of opposition. This was the beginning of a new civil war. Until then, a war had been going on between revolutionary France and the Old Regime; now there was also a war among the revolutionaries.

The moderate majority of the Convention was destroyed. Losing its Girondist leaders, it left Paris and scattered. For nearly two years, not more than two hundred out of 750 deputies sat. It was the end to all discussion. The small minority of Montagnards, which had control of the organized armed bands of the Parisian masses, became masters of the Republic. The right of opposition was more and more limited. Only the Mountain existed now, a minority of the Convention, which in turn represented only a minority of France. Thus, by a fatal link, the government encroached more and more on the rights of the majority. It became even more illegitimate. What a fall in three years from the Estates-General, a true and free expression of France!

How can this extension of illegal power be explained? By the growing fear. The Revolution, because of fear and because it had so little confidence in its own power, began by doing away with the right of opposition by the France of the Old Regime. In order to preserve its illegitimate gains, the Revolution aggravated the situation further by denying the right of opposition even to the members of the Convention. Fear could only grow. The legend of counterrevolution was the vehicle of this fear.

The consequences of the second of June were terrible. The civil war broke out in the heart of revolutionary France. Paris was not only the capital of France, it was also the capital of the Revolution. The revolutionary party there was the strongest. In the departments the moderates dominated, although almost everywhere there was a struggle with the small party of extremists that took its orders from Paris. The resort to force against the majority of the Convention also brought on an enormous emotional reaction in the provinces and generated a movement of solidarity in favor of the arrested Girondist leaders. The moderate elements at the heads of administrations rebelled. They sought to act in concert in the various departments to organize common action against the party that had seized power in Paris. The Convention was threatened by a general revolt in France; only fifteen departments remained outside this conspiracy. The Assembly gave heed to the storm. It sent commissioners everywhere to support the small revolutionary party and by means of terror sought to destroy the moderate majority.

Among them, Fouché and Carrier acquired sinister reputations, the former because of the executions in Lyons, and the latter for the judicial drownings at Nantes.

The Committee of Public Safety and the Convention understood that force alone could not put down the insurrection. It was necessary also to discredit the adversary. The Girondists were accused of federalism, that is, of wishing to transform the state into a federation of small republics and thus disrupt the unity of France to deliver her up to foreign armies. Did this accusation have a basis in fact? Without a doubt, after the declaration of the Republic there was discussion of recasting the political institutions in a federalist direction. This was logical. The French Republic was a complete innovation in Europe. There was no precedent other than the United States of America, which was truly a federation of states. It was quite natural to wish to imitate this example. But there is a great difference between a theoretical discussion of the possibilities of such a project and its practical realization. How could France, which for centuries was a centralized monarchy, become a confederation? Such a transformation would necessitate overcoming insurmountable obstacles.

The Girondists defended themselves by declaring that it was not possible to accuse them at the same time of both federalism and royalism. "If we are royalists," they replied rightly, "we cannot be federalists, because the monarchy is based on a principle of unification; if we are federalists, we can only be republicans." This was a logical argument. Marat himself was convinced. He abandoned the charge of federalism. Nonetheless, it served its purpose at the Convention. It permitted him to pose before the nation as the champion of national unity, a unity which was more necessary than ever, now that France was at war with the rest of Europe.

Dismayed by the terrible situation in which it found itself, the Committee of Public Safety understood the necessity of making a constitution in all haste, and the importance of rallying all the departments. Indeed, the Convention was not a true government. It did not rest on anything, not even a written constitution. The constitution of 1791, having been prepared for a monarchy, had no validity for a republic. Having no legal basis, the Convention was particularly vulnerable. Conscious of its weakness, it had charged a committee to prepare a constitution immediately after the elections. Since nothing had yet been done, the Committee of Public Safety hastily took on the project. It submitted a draft to the Assembly. The constitution, the ratification of which dragged on for eight months, was prepared in thirteen days, from June 11 to June 24.

The constitution of 1793 recognized the people as sovereign. It was the only constitution of the Revolution that had dared to provide for universal suffrage. On the day after the *coup d'état* of June 2, when the government was reduced to an absolute dictatorship of a small oligarchy, this triumph of pure doctrinaire democracy was an extravagant paradox, a violent and chimerical return to revolution. The Constituent Assembly cautiously sought to realize this revolution by establishing popular sovereignty based on a large number of property owners. As a reaction to the last *coup d'état,* the Convention arrived, with one leap, at universal suffrage. But to function properly, universal suffrage required precisely what was nonexistent in 1793: a country in which order reigned, in which parties and classes were not torn apart by violent dissension. Yet this paradox can be explained. It was only one aspect of the contradictions in which the Revolution floundered throughout its history. While completely violating its own principles, the Revolution was unable to deny them. The more it violated them, the more it affirmed them. This was the tragedy. The Revolution was able neither to apply its principles nor to disavow them. This was a terrible misfortune.

The Committee of Public Safety and the Convention hoped that this constitution would restore calm to France, but it only exacerbated passions. The Enragés engaged in a violent campaign against it because of its weakness in dealing with the rise in the cost of living and with the monopolists. The confusion grew worse. New disorders broke out. On July 13, unusual news spread throughout Paris: Marat, the most popular champion of the Revolution, had been assassinated by a young woman of twenty-five, Charlotte Corday.

We have a firsthand document concerning Charlotte Corday, an article by Casimir Périer, published in the *Revue des Deux-Mondes,* in which he tells of having known a certain Madame de M., who was a friend of Charlotte Corday and who enjoyed her confidence. Madame de M. wrote her reminiscences of Charlotte Corday and gave them to Périer to be published after her death. It was this brief manuscript which appeared in the *Revue de Deux-Mondes*.

Charlotte, who was very pretty, was completely lacking in coquettishness. She was a devout Catholic. She had never desired to read a page of Voltaire or Rousseau, whose works had been interdicted by the Church. She was not a royalist, as was the rest of her family, but a republican of Girondist leanings. She had a literary infatuation for ancient Rome, its austere virtues and heroism. She was behind the times, a distant child of Corneille. She was teased for being pedantic and citing Roman examples. She said that she did not wish to marry because she did not want to give up her liberty. When she killed Marat, it was said that she sought to avenge her lover. "Charlotte Corday; a lover," said her friend. "Impossible."

When arrested, she displayed the most heroic stoicism. At her trial she said that she was certain she had done her duty in killing Marat; it was the only way to save France. She was condemned to the gallows. Clothed in the red robe of a murderer, she was led through Paris standing in a cart. She was calm in front of a mob that shouted insults at her, and she died with great dignity. Her death produced a profound impression. The Committee of General Safety complained that there was too much talk of this "extraordinary" woman; it was necessary to try to forget her.

The assassination of Marat was testimony of the profound split within France. The assault upon the Girondists has been a shock to all France, and Charlotte Corday became the expression of collective resentment. The Terror began with the death of Marat. The revolutionary leaders now felt themselves in danger. Until then, few of them had died a violent death, but now the victim of violence had been the leader of the extremist party.

The constitution, which was voted by the Convention in June, was approved by a vote of 1,800,000 to 11,000 in a referendum held in July. Less than a third of the seven million eligible to vote had done so, and within that third, there was no opposition to speak of. This was further proof that the Republic was the government of a unanimous, more or less sincere minority that had usurped the role of the sovereign people, thanks to a spurious "refinement" of universal suffrage. There was an obvious contradiction, as indicated by the figures, between the doctrine and its realization in practice.

It only remained to put the constitution into operation, that is, to hold an election based on universal suffrage, form a new government, and transfer power to it. But the new constitution had scarcely been proclaimed when the Jacobins demanded that it be put off and the powers of the Convention be continued until the end of the war. The Revolution could continue without violating its principles only if it denied them.

The difficulty of providing food became ever greater. The district of Gros-Caillou took the initiative by establishing "bread cards." It was proposed that this be done everywhere. Each citizen would have to state to a citizens' committee in his district his name, residence, and the number of those he had to feed. This information would be noted on a card, and upon presentation of it, the baker in the arrondissement would be required to furnish the bearer with a specified amount of bread. It was the first appearance of ration cards.

At the same time that the nation was faced with the danger both of invasion and of famine, the idea of *levée en masse* and of a general requisition of foodstuffs spread among the revolutionary groups. This suggestion, before which the men in power drew back, loomed large among the masses. It was put forward by an obscure individual, Sébastien Lacroix, in a speech that was immediately published under the significant title, *Not a Moment to Lose.* It was an immense success. On August 12, a deputation of Jacobin leaders proposed that the Convention enact such a measure. On the fourteenth, the Committee of Public Safety gave its support to a decree that delegated eighteen representatives in the departments to organize a *levée en masse* "for the requisition of men, arms, supplies, forage, and horses." The final decree was voted on August 23. This resulted in general requisitioning of wealth and the produce of labor.

By February, the drafting of 300,000 men had not resolved the military problem. There was still a dearth of officers, arms, horses, equipment, and money. With the admission of Carnot and Prieur of the Côte d'Or to the Committee of Public Safety on August 14, the organization of the army received a strong impetus. Recruitment did not provoke the resistance which had been occasioned by the drafting of 300,000 men, whether because there was a realization of the national peril or because of increased unemployment and distress. By becoming a soldier, one was at least assured of lodgings and food and modest pay. Arms factories were opened throughout the country and especially in Paris. Palaces were requisitioned for this purpose. All the blacksmiths were mobilized for the war industries. Activities of a different nature became the object of concern of the Convention: the preservation of monuments, reforms of weights and measures, etc.

Where was this surge of energy coming from? It came from the second revolution, which was beginning at this time and which would work to create a totalitarian state in France. It was during July, August, and September, 1793, that the first seed appeared in Paris under the threat of invasion, a seed that grew and developed over the next twenty years, through crises and violent storms. This new revolution had nothing in common with the revolution of 1789. It was a complete denial of the right of opposition and led to the destruction of all political liberties. The woes caused by the French Revolution were the consequence of this second revolution, the basis of which is to be found in the destruction of the monarchical legitimacy.

It is because the two revolutions have been confused that the history of the French Revolution has become an unintelligible jumble. And it is this lack of understanding which is still one of the principal causes of the confusion, for a century and a half, in the political ideas of Europe. Is it not the origin of the catastrophe of which we ourselves are the victims? In order to understand what is happening today, it is very important to look clearly at these two revolutions, for they both pose a major problem that must be resolved by the Western world. Proof that this problem exists can be found in the totally different judgments regarding the second revolution expressed by two illustrious historians, Taine and Jaurès. Here is how Taine defined the revolutionary government:

> On August 24, upon the motion of Basire, the Convention decreed "that France is in a state of revolution until its independence is recognized." This signified that the period of hypocritical phrases was over; that the constitution was only a showpiece; that there was no need to pretend otherwise; that the posters with the old slogans were stored away; that private and public liberties, local as well as parliamentary, were abolished. That the government was arbitrary and absolute; that no institution, law, principle, dogma, or precedent was a guaranty, against the government, of the rights either of the individual or of the people as a whole; that all property and lives are at its discretion; that the rights of man no longer existed....
>
> This regime, brought into being by Saint-Juste, was like an oligarchy of invaders which maintains itself over a subjugated nation. By such a system, ten thousand Spartans were able in Greece, after the Dorian invasions, to become masters of 300,000 helots and Perioeci. So were 300,000 Jacobins in France

able to become masters of six or seven million Girondists, Feuillants, royalists, and those who were indifferent to politics.

This is what Jaurès wrote:

Never, since the Revolution, had Paris reflected such energy, unity, luster, and serene expectation as after the elimination of the Gironde.

One of the two must be wrong—unless both are correct, which is also possible. This contradiction occurs among writers, historians, philosophers, and sociologists of all countries. It is to be found only in a profoundly divided society that has lost the sense of fundamental principles essential to social order. It is necessary, therefore, to search for the real origin of this convulsion and to seek to understand why, for a century and a half, the same event gave rise to such differing judgments.

Five conditions are necessary for the formation of a revolutionary state.

1. A disruption of the former legal system is the first condition. In France this break was complete. But it need not be that complete. In Germany, for example, following the war of 1914–1918, the monarchy fell but the bureaucracy survived, which did not prevent the formation of a revolutionary state. In Italy, a weakening of the monarchy was sufficient.

2. Illegitimate power is the second condition. It is a consequence of the first. In an illegitimate government, the right to command is not recognized by the majority

and is imposed by force. Only sincere acceptance, whether active or passive, can make power legitimate.

3. A general state of fear is the third condition. It follows upon the break with legality and the illegitimacy of power. Those who should obey are afraid of those in power, and those in power fear those whom they must command.

4. Abuse of force. If to this fear is added war and an economic crisis such as existed in France, the situation is aggravated. What is the result? The use of force. There is no longer any recognized limit to power and it becomes absolute. This is the critical point of all revolutions. The illegitimate government is seized by fear, and fear brings it to the abuse of its power. Since it fears the victims of these abuses, far from being cured the fear grows and brings on even greater abuse. We enter into a vicious circle: fear provokes abuse of power, and the abuse of power increases the fear. By itself, the revolution never succeeds in breaking out of this circle.

5. A morbid excess of energy. As a legitimate regime grows old, its traditions, principles, and laws crystallize, and its functioning becomes more certain but its spirit of initiative becomes more limited. It is difficult for it to detach itself from its laws, its principles, and its traditions. A revolutionary state, on the contrary, has broken its framework and enjoys a certain liberty. It has much greater scope to experiment. At times the innovations are terrible; at times they are useful innovations that legitimate governments adopt at a later date.

These five principles are the key to the history of the French Revolution until 1814, and to the current state of affairs in Europe. The government was stricken with a morbid energy and exceeded the limits which prudence, tradition, and common sense impose on the actions of those in power. The new republic was to transform itself with increasing speed into the dictatorship of a small oligarchy, and power was to fall into the hands of even smaller minorities, which became increasingly more violent. They were prisoners in a vicious circle of fear. The foreign peril, which grew more threatening each day, added to the fear of this minority government and pushed it to even more violent measures. Fear multiplied suspicion; suspicions aggravated hatred and discord; hatred and discord divided the government minority into ever smaller segments, which exterminated each other. Those who survived, more diminished and more terrorized than were their predecessors, carried the process even further. It was a chain which no human force could break.

On August 28, Barrère, on behalf of the Committee of Public Safety, declared in the Convention: " 'Moderatism' dampens the enthusiasm of the people and secretly promotes the counterrevolution." What was "moderatism"? The ability to resort to power intelligently and with moderation. But now the intelligent use of force was officially regarded as a form of counterrevolution. On September 5, a deputation from the forty-eight districts demanded that terror be made the order of the day. Barrère appropriated this formula in the name of the

Committee of Public Safety, and the Terror, the final convulsion of the Great Fear, began.

The special criminal tribunal took the name of Revolutionary Tribunal and multiplied its activities. Similar tribunals were constituted in the provinces. The laws against the émigrés, the nobles, and the clergy were applied with savage severity. Prosecutions mounted. On October 10, on the motion of the Committee of Public Safety, the Convention decreed that the provisional revolutionary government of France would continue until peace was attained. They expected that the situation would be temporary. But that was an illusion. How escape the vicious circle of the state in revolution?

PART II

The Second Revolution

CHAPTER 1
The Revolutionary Government

The Convention continued to meet after the elimination, on June 2, of the Girondists, but it represented only a minority of a minority. As the sovereign authority, it made the laws and named the members of, and supervised, the Committee of Public Safety, the principal organ of executive power. It was an illegitimate government not only because it had been elected by a reduced electorate but because it had been illegal from the beginning. It could maintain itself only by force.

Along with the Convention, the municipality of Paris constituted another sovereign authority of the second degree; it, too, was illegitimate since it was established as a result of an uprising. However, it was not a negligible force. It organized armed bands of Parisian workers, and since, under the constitution, the municipality exercised the direction of the National Guard, it controlled the entire armed force.

Another troublesome force was the Jacobin club. It had branches all over the country and it exercised great influence over the municipality of Paris and the Convention, whose actions it upheld in the provinces.

In all three organs the Mountain dominated, even though it was itself a minority. But it was far from united. It was divided into three groups, which, without having markedly different or well-defined programs, were united behind three leaders, Hébert, Danton, and Robespierre, each of whom had his own supporters. As for the mob, which was more unstable, it attached itself now to one, now to the other. During the autumn of 1793, the Hébertist group predominated. It gave an extremely violent character to the ideas of the Mountain. Partisan of a war to the end, it demanded the extermination of the nobles, and a war against the rich and against the monopolists. Its headquarters was the club of the Cordeliers. Its chief, Hébert, was from a family of ruined merchants, which had prevented him from pursuing a normal career. He worked at many occupations before throwing himself into the Revolution. He took an active part in the struggle against the Girondists, and even had been imprisoned, a fact which brought him great popularity after June 2.

The movement that he directed was characterized by a phenomenon, common to all revolutions, which the Italians call "turpiloquio," that is, the use of obscene language. Here, for example, are several lines about Marie-Antoinette taken from Hébert's newspaper, *Le Père Duchêne:*

The Austrian tigress is looked upon in all the courts of Europe as the most wretched prostitute in France. She has been openly accused of sprawling in the dirt with her footmen and one is at a loss to single out the camp followers who have helped to produce the crippled, deformed, and gangrenous miserable specimens emerging from her wrinkled belly.

This kind of language was an appeal to the savage passions unleashed by fear. The people of Paris would never have listened, had they not been obsessed with the fear of counterrevolution.

It was during this time that a series of innovations were embarked upon, another characteristic of revolutionary states. The form of address "monsieur" was replaced by "citoyen"; the familiar address replaced the polite one. Another change was in dress. One of the most important changes was in the basic attitude toward Christianity. Before this, the Revolution had attacked the Church, but not religion; now sacrilegious parodies and blasphemous masquerades were organized by the Hébertists. Jesus became a sans-culotte. So that no one would have to bear the name of a saint, names were borrowed from the Greeks and the Romans. A new calendar was adopted which abolished Sundays and religious holidays. The new year began on September 21, the date of the founding of the Republic.

The most typical manifestation of this political anti-religiosity was the Festival of Liberty, celebrated on November 10, 1793, in Notre Dame de Paris, in which an actress from the Opéra represented Reason. Torches were lighted and speeches delivered. The representatives of the Commune and the department went before the Convention and declared that the people wanted no other gods but nature. Then the churches were transformed into temples of Reason. On November 23, the Commune of Paris, upon the motion of Chaumette, decreed the closing of all churches in Paris, "in view of the fact that the people of Paris have declared that they recognize no other creed than that of Truth and Reason."

What was the significance of these demonstrations against traditional religion? This was, basically, a means for the Hébertists to revive for themselves and for others the feeling of being a revolutionary force. This is common to all revolutions. Those who have been successful in an uprising against a legal government attempt to instill the belief that they are able to make significant changes for the collective good in the established order of centuries. That is why revolutionary governments indulge in spectacular quackery. This explains their actions and conduct, though they have been interpreted quite differently.

In a country where for centuries the Church had been

158

the object of official and popular veneration, the sacrilegious carnivals of the Hébertists could not fail to make a strong impression. In the state of impotence the Church was in, they brought few consequences, however, and they involved little danger. But this political anti-religiosity was the origin of the opposition of the Hébertists to the Dantonists and to the Robespierrists. Robespierre was especially hostile. He dreamed of a reform that would replace Catholicism with a Rousseauesque civic religion. The burlesques of the Hébertists disgusted him. He was perfectly aware that they scandalized the Catholics and equally displeased those who were outside the Church. The freethinkers themselves had a certain respect for a religion that had played so considerable a role in the development of Western civilization.

Until the crushing of the Girondists, the government had observed a measure of revolutionary legality. The abuses of force had been limited. But after June 2 these abuses multiplied. To satisfy the people, the Convention approved a law on July 26 which punished by death anyone who monopolized basic necessities. It is important to understand the dangers of such a measure.

Commerce is a vital regulator of economic life precisely because it monopolizes. A merchant cannot buy goods every day. In stocking merchandise, he helps to regulate the market. When a product is in short supply, he raises the price to limit its sale; when it becomes abundant, he lowers the price. The regulatory function of commerce on the market is extremely useful. It was endangered by the law of the Convention. Merchants were obliged to make inventories of their merchandise. If any one of them wished to sell his goods immediately to anyone, he could continue his trade; if not, the state would take over. This was nationalization of commerce. The French Revolution had set the example precisely because this is one of the expedients of revolutionary governments.

On September 17, the Convention authorized the immediate arrest of all suspects. There followed a veritable frenzy of persecution. The more violence increased, the more the government feared a revolt. Incited by fear, and in an attempt to prevent the rise in prices, the Convention ended by voting, on September 29, the Law of the Maximum on basic commodities. Conscious of the uselessness and dangers of such a measure, it had long hesitated to take this step. However, the masses invoked the maximum as the supreme good. The government, fearing that the masses would cease to support the Revolution, felt obliged to satisfy them. A maximum price was fixed for certain commodities, and other prices were increased by a third over the prices current in 1790. Prices were not the same throughout France, however, and commodities varied greatly in price from one department to the other.

This law had immediate repercussions. Following a long speech by Saint-Just, the Convention, as has been noted, had decreed on October 10 that, until peace was proclaimed, the government of France was to remain revolutionary. This was the official designation. From certain passages in the speech of Saint-Just it is possible to understand the extreme tension brought on by the use of force. An illegitimate government, to maintain itself in power, arrogates to itself the right to use force to the limit. Saint-Just declared that the Law of the Maximum would not be effective unless it were applied implacably, and he proposed the creation of extraordinary tribunals to compel the rich merchants to obey the law. He ended his speech with a virulent appeal for violence.

The result was an intensification of fear. The statistics of those imprisoned in Paris is evidence enough: 1,182 on June 1; 1,794 on September 8; 2,378 on October 5; 3,235 on November 17; 4,325 on December 24. This was a veritable progression of Terror. In the autumn of 1793, executions reached some ten a day. And these were few compared to what was to come. To prepare the way for new uses of force, the masses were held in suspense with spectacular trials. The three most famous were those of General Custine, of Marie-Antoinette, and of the Girondists.

Custine commanded the Army of the North which had lost Valenciennes. He was accused of treason, and his case was referred to the Revolutionary Tribunal. The tribunal hesitated to condemn him, however. Would not the passing of the death penalty for a lost battle deprive the generals of the *sang-froid* that is so essential to a commander? Who would then risk assuming command of an army? Nevertheless, under popular pressure, Custine was condemned and executed.

On October 16 it was Marie-Antoinette's turn. Robespierre and Danton would have prevented her trial. The war with England had been an outcome of the trial of Louis XVI. Why begin another war in the same way? However, by the basest of calumnies, the Hébertists successfully inflamed the masses against the queen and secured approval for her sentencing. The Habsburgs did nothing to save her. But her sister, Marie-Caroline, Queen of Naples, henceforth felt an implacable hatred for the Revolution which later cost France dearly. When Lord Nelson lost his way while crossing the Mediterranean in search of the French fleet, Marie-Caroline showed him where the fleet was. Abukir was the funeral sacrifice she offered to the shade of her sister.

The most serious of these trials was that of the Girondists. The indictment was to have been presented by the Committee of General Security, but strong opposition developed in the committee and the indictment was never drawn up. The revolts in Toulouse and in Lyons precipitated the trial, however. The Girondists were accused of being responsible, which was to a certain degree true. The majority of the Convention was carried along, and the case of the twenty-nine Girondist deputies was brought before the Revolutionary Tribunal. All legal defense was denied them. Accused of conspiracy against the integrity and unity of the Republic, they were executed on October 31.

Meanwhile, as its adversaries had foreseen, the Law of the Maximum, far from resolving the economic problem, only aggravated it further and led to the disappearance altogether of many articles of merchandise. Such a confused and intolerable state of affairs did not arouse any opposition. Robespierrists and Dantonists did not dare raise any protest, though they were opposed to the Law of the Maximum. Here was clear proof of the weakness of the government, which claimed to be democratic! A democratic government makes no sense without an active opposition. And with the elimination of the Girondists, all opposition disappeared from the Convention. Very important laws were passed with almost no discussion, despite the opposition of the majority. After the country entered the ultra-revolutionary phase, intimidation replaced deliberation. There were various methods of intimidation: press campaigns, demonstrations in the galleries of the Convention hall, and acts of violence, for the armed forces in Paris were under the control of the Hébertists. These methods were used against anyone who wished to express opposition, however reasonably. All opposition was considered counterrevolutionary. Such a charge, leveled while the Revolutionary Tribunal was functioning regularly, was enough to frighten the best of men. Danton was particularly vulnerable to a charge of this nature, as he had openly declared that the war must be brought to an end. It was also alleged that Danton contemplated the restoration of the monarchy. Though proof was lacking, the assumption was probably true, for, with the exception of Robespierre, a republican *enragé,* all the others—even Hébert—had at times envisaged a return to the monarchy as the only recourse. Twenty years later, history was to prove them right.

To discredit a majority of the Assembly, Hébert demanded the implementation of the new constitution and the calling of elections. Henceforth, he refused to recognize the authority of the Convention. Legally, he was right. It was doubtlessly because the extreme revolutionary party expected to gain a majority in the new elections, however, that it became the champion of constitutional legality.

The Dantonist and Robespierrist majority replied to the accusation of the Hébertists that it was the Hébertists themselves who, in carrying matters to an extreme, were rendering inevitable the restoration of the monarchy in agreement with Pitt. This propaganda was supported by a skillful opposition that claimed that the evils the people were suffering were not the result of the laws that had been voted, which were in principle good, but were due to the way the laws were applied by the party in power.

The economic discontent and the growing horror of the Terror were the two principal tools of the opposition. This regime of denunciation and endless condemnations spread a general dissatisfaction which the opposition sought to exploit against the party of Hébert. A group demanding the end of the Terror split with the Dantonists. Robespierre would also have inclined to be more indulgent. He was not so implacable as history has represented him. He was opposed to the sentencing of Marie-Antoinette and of Madame Elisabeth, the king's sister. These acts of violence seemed to him useless domestically and very dangerous from a foreign point of view. However, more prudent than Danton, he never compromised himself in favor of a policy of clemency. Influenced by

164

The Revolutionary Government

Danton, Camille Desmoulins took as an example the despotism of Rome to demand, in the *Vieux Cordelier,* the end of the Terror.

There was no reason for the Hébertists to end the policy of intimidation. The more disastrous the effects of the laws they had passed, the greater the irritation of the members of the Convention at having been coerced into voting for them. The more the Hébertists emphasized intimidation in order to avoid an outbreak of violent opposition, the more the majority was incensed. The situation in the Convention in the winter of 1793 was this: a small minority was imposing its terrorist laws by intimidation and accusation; and the majority was in a state of latent and growing revolt.

Mutual suspicion made life untenable. The illegitimate character of the government was mainly responsible. For a regular opposition to function in a representative government, it is necessary that power be firmly established, that the right to command be accepted, and that a reasonable policy exist which would raise no objections other than those that ordinary logic would suggest. All of this was lacking in 1793. That is why life became intolerable. The group in power feared a revolt and, to prevent it, abused its power, which only increased the fear and aggravated the situation.

Is this explanation valid? It is a problem of critical importance. The same situation has recurred in Europe, and we must determine its cause. Otherwise, Europe is destined to vanish from the civilized world.

Albert Mathiez has offered another explanation. Since

165

he is professor of the history of the French Revolution at the Sorbonne, his interpretation has become the official doctrine in France. In his work *Robespierre terroriste,* he holds that the Terror was caused by the war and the threat of invasion; that it was this external factor, not an internal one such as the illegitimacy of power, which was responsible. The Terror, according to him, was an anticipation of what France was to experience during World War I when she declared a state of siege—and he goes on to give a vivid picture of the period. Without doubt, during World War I, France submitted to a policy of coercion which was necessary because of the war. The proof that it was really an external cause that led to the establishment of such a regime is that it disappeared immediately after the termination of the war, when there was a return to the ordinary forms of government, with all the guarantees that a civilized state can assure to its subjects. The cause having disappeared, the effect disappeared too.

However, in the second half of 1793 an opposite situation developed. The military position of France improved rapidly and the danger of invasion was removed. With the exception of Valenciennes and Condé, all French territory was liberated. Lyons and Toulon, which had revolted, were recaptured, and the insurrection in the Vendée was crushed. If the state of war was the essential cause of the Terror, the improvement in the military situation should have correspondingly led to an amelioration of the internal regime. Since exactly the opposite occurred, the inescapable conclusion is that the military situation was not the sole cause. Far from disappearing, the Terror spread to the army. Despite the victories, there occurred a kind of strike by army officers. Suspicions and complaints multiplied to such an extent that officers no longer wished to have command. Discipline was affected, and Robespierre denounced the growing number of acts of treachery. This was in December 1793, in the midst of military success! The root of evil was not external; it lay not in the threat of the Allied armies but internally, in the manner in which the government was organized and in the principles that were enunciated to justify its authority.

It was impossible to continue in this fashion. In 1794, a plan was conceived to exterminate at the same time both the Hébertist group on the Left and the Dantonist group on the Right, and to create with the center a stable government capable of governing France.

Where did the initiative for this project come from? Historians have not asked this, for they have thought that the situation was clear. For a long time, in effect, they believed that Robespierre was responsible for the important decisions: that it was his idea to purge the parties of both the Left and the Right, or at least to suppress them by means of the Revolutionary Tribunal and the gallows. When, under a revolutionary regime, the opposition is not able to make itself heard, the differences are decided by slaughter.

Documents found at the end of the nineteenth century lead us to believe that it was the Abbé Sieyès who conceived of this purge and had it executed by Robespierre. When asked what he did during the Terror, Sieyès replied, "I survived": that is, escaped death. He would have pretended not to have even known Robespierre. The documents which cast doubt on the allegations against Robespierre are taken from the archives of Lord Grenville, who was the British Minister of Foreign Affairs during this period. It was a private correspondence in which are found twenty-eight reports in French dating from September 2, 1793, to June 22, 1794. These reports, sent from Paris by a secret informer, consist of notes on the deliberations of the Committee of Public Safety. Whereas the official reports of the committee only give the decisions of the committee, these reports contain detailed accounts of the preceding discussions. The first of these reports was sent to Lord Grenville by Drake, the English minister to Genoa, with a letter advising secrecy.

What credence can be given these reports? Aulard speaks of them as mystifying. Historians, who should look favorably on documents that can throw new light on important events, are men like any others and have great difficulty in renouncing fixed opinions. Mathiez himself did not share Aulard's sentiments. His researches enabled him to establish that the Committee of Public Safety had knowledge of the existence of the first report. It had fallen into the hands of Las Casas, Spanish ambassador to Venice, who was in close contact with a French diplomat in Constantinople, Hénin, with whom he kept up a correspondence (addressed to his "dear enemy") despite the fact that a state of war existed between France and Spain. The first report indicated that there had been a violent discussion in the Committee of Public Safety concerning the funds which had been voted for the purpose of bribing foreign diplomats but which had vanished into the pockets of French agents to whom they had been sent. Indeed, Hénin was among the agents accused. Las Casas immediately warned his friend, who found himself in a painful predicament. If he wanted to clear himself, he would have to reveal his source of information. He resigned himself to this and sent the Committee of Public Safety the letter which he had received and asked if in truth he was being accused; if so, he was ready to defend himself. This was how the Committee of Public Safety learned that someone was betraying its secret deliberations. The members were quite frightened, which gives credence to the belief that the report was not pure invention.

Mathiez also attempted to identify the source of the reports. According to him, they came from Verona, the residence of the future Louis XVIII, and it was Louis XVIII's secretary, the Count of Antraigues, who drafted them, based on the reports he received from the royalists in Paris, and then distributed them afterward to all the chancelleries of Europe. These are only conjectures; but the supposition that the reports were in fact composed by someone in the entourage of the brother of Louis XVI would be further reason to accept their credibility; his intelligence and superior mind would be sufficient guarantee.

These reports belong to a genre of historical documentation based on secret information and indiscretion which contains unavoidably a mixture of truth and falsehood. The possibility that the reports were written by a member of the Committee of Public Safety must be ruled out. It was probably someone in Louis's entourage. Men do not have the power of complete dissimulation. The most jealously guarded secrets often end by being uncovered, at least partially. However, the man who informs a third party of what he has learned is obliged to complete with guesswork the fragments of truth that he possesses. Hence the difficulty of separating in documents of this genre what is and what is not true.

Here, to begin, are several passages from the fourteenth report, sent from Paris on March 9:

On the 7th the Committee of Public Safety remained in session the entire day . . . [following are the decrees passed] . . . Despite this, the Committee has given proof of its weakness by not daring to denounce the Cordelier Club which is boldly conspiring to overthrow it and announces that there will be a great uprising on May 21 [this must have been an error, it was certainly May 31]. There is no doubt that the municipality and the Cordeliers will not triumph over their enemies, and we are sure that Pichégru and Hoche belong to the Cordelier party. If that party were to triumph, what is certain is that the rest of the royal family will be massacred as well as all prisoners.

On the night of the 7th, the Committee of Public Safety expressly charged Robespierre with denouncing at the Convention Hébert, Chaumette, the Municipality, and the Cor-

delier Club as being in league with the coalition powers in order to slaughter the Convention and deliver France to the tyrants. Our friends in Paris were quite convinced on the 8th that neither Robespierre nor any of his colleagues would dare to attempt to take so desperate and hazardous a step.

This last paragraph reflects the real situation, not as represented by the historians, but as it emerges from an objective study. This purge was not the consequence of an uprising; there is nothing to lead to the belief that the Hébertists wanted to resume the action that the extremists had taken against the Girondists on May 31. There was only the fear of such action. The majority of the Convention, the Robespierrists and the Dantonists, feared a new uprising by the Hébertists and the Municipality. This was only a hypothetical fear, however, which would have been justified if it had been up to the Cordeliers. But nothing was attempted.

From the fifteenth report, sent on March 15:

On the night of the 9th, Robespierre and the Abbé Sieyès retired to Choisy together with their chief supporters. . . .

There was an attempt to reconcile the two opposing parties:

The reconciliation between the two opposing parties was not of long duration. All the conditions were faithfully fulfilled by Robespierre, but from the 13th, Hébert, without specifically mentioning Robespierre, lashed out furiously against Barrère, Chabot, and what he called the faction. He attacked the report of Saint-Just on what took place at the meeting of the Cordelier Club and the alleged plot which he had denounced.

Both sides sought to achieve a *rapprochement,* but without success, as neither side was able to overcome its fear. It was because of fear that the Dantonists and the Robespierrists accused the Hébertists of plotting. The Hébertists, in turn, became immediately suspicious; they were afraid, because they believed that the others were denouncing an alleged plot in order to justify their own. The seventeenth report, of March 21, explains how the decision to arrest the Hébertists was reached and reveals the role played by Sieyès:

It has been definitely ascertained that there was a meeting at Choisy on March 12 at which Robespierre, the Abbé Sieyès, and Couthon were present . . . and Mayor Pache, who, while a member or pretending to be a member of the Hébertists, discovered the plans of Hébert. On the 13th . . . a meeting of the Committee of Public Safety was quickly called. It was confirmed that Robespierre as well as Couthon wished to abandon their party and save themselves by going to North America. Only the Abbé Sieyès was opposed; the destruction of the Hébertist faction was his doing. He spoke for more than two hours before the Committee on the morning of March 13. His speech was an attempt to prove to the Committee that the English intelligence in Paris had created this new faction . . . ; that the Committee must remember that the categorical refusal of Mr. Pitt continued to be the prime obstacle to peace, and that this was so because of the weakness resulting from the factions of the French government. If the government of France had a stable base and its authority was certain, England would have to deal with France.

It was indeed so. Sieyès was correct when he said that the greatest difficulty confronting France was its inability to conclude a peace because of Pitt's mistrust of revolutionary governments. It is impossible to negotiate with a government that does not inspire one's confidence. Upon this basic truth Sieyès applied himself to fashion a plan that would overcome the fear. It was true that England did not want a republic in France, on the grounds that a republic would be unstable and would threaten the balance of power in Europe. But Sieyès was wrong in thinking that there was an agreement between Hébert and Pitt to conclude a peace over the ruins of the Republic. There is no proof of this, though it is undoubtedly a twisting of a more profound truth. Hébert saw the necessity of establishing a more powerful government capable of negotiating with England. The same thought ran through the opposing camps.

All this is only to be expected in a revolutionary government. Moreover, one can understand why Sieyès was concerned about a possible restoration of the monarchy. Having transformed the Estates-General into the Constituent Assembly, he was seriously compromised in the eyes of royalty.

On March 14, every careful observer was perfectly convinced that nowhere else in all the universe was there a people more susceptible to being overcome by fear than the bour-

geoisie and the people of Paris. If ever the army of the coalition were to approach Paris, it would not be despair that one would observe in this city, but fear and only fear. On the morning of the 14th, the Convention was as alarmed as it is possible to be, because of the arrests that were about to take place and the effects that would be produced upon the people who lived or met at the Cordeliers. The Jacobins were surrounded by their partisans in their club, and it wasn't until they knew that the Cordelier Club had taken fright and had fled that the triumphant party resumed its ferocity.

The situation could not have been better described. The Convention became frightened by what it had dared to undertake against its adversaries. It was reassured only when it learned that the enemy was even more frightened than it was.

Following is part of the eighteenth report, dated March 28:

On the 24th, all the leaders of the Hébertist party were guillotined. On the 22nd and 23rd, there had been some negotiation with the Committee of Public Safety to save their lives and confine them to prison instead, but this hope was short-lived. It originated in the turmoil that was noted among the people who openly asserted that the plot was an invention of Robespierre. The latter, being troubled, yielded to Hébert's proposal to examine the truth of the charges. This would accord Hébert a delay and permit him to escape. On the 23rd, however, Robespierre distributed 800,000 livres in assignats among the people. This produced the desired effect: there was no further question about Hébert's proposal.

This was all quite likely. We see it also in the trials in Russia. When one political faction wishes to rid itself of another, it lashes out with a false accusation, assuring itself by obtaining the confession of the accused.

Here are two interesting and historically accurate judgments, the first concerning Robespierre:

Robespierre was not a man of courage or of great talent. He was able to achieve what he did, because while his colleagues in the first Constituent Assembly and the Legislature Assembly shifted their stratagems to bring the people by degrees to their point of view, he constantly refuted these stratagems. From the first year of the Revolution he professed democracy pure and simple, as he does now. Thus, he would never bring himself to make the Revolution step by step as his colleagues did by following the masses. He believed that what is achieved would have to be achieved immediately and that, the Revolution accomplished, he would attain great popularity. To keep it was neither in his power nor in his character; he was too insolent; and without the Abbé Sieyès, who was greatly attached to him, he would long since have lost all influence.

And here is the judgment concerning the Abbé Sieyès:

The Abbé Sieyès, the most evil man who has ever existed, is surely the most resourceful and most ferocious man France has ever seen. He doesn't want to seize power personally, but he wishes to rule over those whom by his counsel he will lead to the attainment of supreme authority. He has found this in Robespierre, but certainly he will not find it in Saint-Just. The Abbé Sieyès is convinced, and he has made no secret of this for the past three years, that the reign of kings in Europe is over; that a century of anarchy must ensue everywhere, after which, he says, we will see the birth of new institutions. Therefore, he will never in good faith accept any proposal of accommodation with any sovereign. . . . Meanwhile he has declared to the Committee several times that if it is necessary to call a halt to the war, he does not oppose a truce, since he feels that it will be more disastrous for the kings than dangerous to the Republic.

A remarkable judgment! Whoever made it, understood human nature well. It is an exaggeration to represent Sieyès as the most evil man in the world. It is true that he inspired much antipathy. He was certainly dry, hard, and arrogant, but he was also courageous and capable of making decisions. He proved it in 1789 and was to prove it again in 1799. It is correct to say that he did not seek power for himself; he aspired to control those who held it. It was to him that Napoleon owed his rise. If Sieyès's plan to make Napoleon his creature was not entirely successful, it did not completely miscarry either. During the Consulate and the first years of the Empire, Sieyès exerted great influence. The ideas which the report ascribes to him concerning the political situation seem to have been drawn from a good source. They are remarkably profound. Likewise, he probably played the role attributed to him. What we know of Sieyès confirms this. The vacillation of Robespierre also seems likely. Even those revolutionaries who seem most energetic often act out of fear. It is much easier for someone who is not in the public eye, like

Sieyès, to be courageous. Our great difficulty in accepting the fact that he did play this role comes from this: for a long time we did not know of his acquaintance with Robespierre. Indeed, the Abbé declared publicly that he did not know him. As strange as this may seem, it is not unreasonable. Sieyès was a prudent and a patient man. Not long after the fall of Robespierre, he reappeared on the political scene. He probably had remained apart out of fear of being suspected. Many of those who might have known of his relationship with Robespierre during the Terror were already dead. Then, after the fall of Robespierre, the Convention settled down with a new constitution. Sieyès, who was considered a specialist in constitutional matters, did not make any public appearances at this time. Without doubt, he had reasons to let himself be forgotten. Was not the role he had played in 1794 one of those reasons?

It is certain that the trial instituted against the Hébertists was an attempt by the Committee of Public Safety to get out of an impossible situation. This was the first trial which the Revolution had deliberately planned for the purpose of radically altering the political situation. The decision to try the Girondists had been arrived at only by degrees. Now the whole thing was planned, from the very beginning. Hébert and his friends were arrested together with several persons not associated with them, such as Anacharsis Cloots, the Rhenish visionary who dreamed of a universal republic and of revolutionary war against all the kings of Europe. Such a program could hardly please the Committee of Public Safety, which was sufficiently occupied with the struggle with England and the empire. The Committee took advantage of the trial of the Hébertists to rid itself of the particular danger. The friends of Dumouriez, as well as several foreigners implicated in carrying on intelligence with the enemy, were also arrested.

The trial was a cruel travesty. The defendants were indicted on the charge of plotting to starve Paris, to destroy the Convention, and to establish a dictatorship. No serious proof could be produced, and the charges were dropped during the course of the trial. The witnesses testified only as to the political conduct and private morals of the accused. Demonstrations also were organized against the Hébertists. They had counted among them several popular parties, but now that their chiefs were imprisoned and they were leaderless, the Committee of Public Safety proceeded to take them in hand. The Hébertists were condemned to death for having wished to "dissolve the national representative body, to assassinate its members and the patriots, to destroy the republican government, to deprive the people of their sovereignty, and to set up a tyrannical state." They were executed on the same day, March 24, 1794. Despite the efforts of the Committee of Public Safety, the trial left a most unfortunate impression. The Hébertists had many sympathizers among the people of Paris, who considered them the champions of the Revolution and who knew how unfounded the indictment against them was.

178

The Revolutionary Government

These executions [wrote Jaurès] greatly confused the people. A small number of persons persisted in believing, even after the trial, that the condemned were innocent. The majority said, "Whom can we trust now? Will we always be fooled? The moderates are suspect; and the extremists are traitors who seek to deceive us."

The Committee of Public Safety was vigilant and took vigorous action. However, one has the impression that, so as not to be outdone by the conspirators, the Committee was obliged to regulate trifles, to stress the evils, to transform into a fully hatched plot, waiting to be set off, what were only vague dreams of overexcited souls. This sickness extended, in one way or another, throughout all social strata, to the heart of the revolutionary consciousness, and had a corrupting influence on the recollections of the revolutionaries and the pious admiration of the people. Finally, those who were about to mount the scaffold said they were Maratists. . . . Was Marat also part of the conspiracy? These fine gentlemen spread rumors to distract the revolutionary piety of the people and, by raising doubts, to quench the revolutionary fire. The partisans of Hébert also whispered these things in order to confuse Hébertism with Maratism.

This is correct. The Committee of Public Safety found itself between two fires: the Catholic and royalist opposition on the one hand, and the Hébertists on the other. Both repeat the same argument, that it is not a conspiracy which they wanted to foil, but revolutionary extremism which they wanted to stamp out. The situation became so difficult that the Committee of Public Safety sought to extricate itself by a new uprising. To satisfy the extreme

Left, it sought to attack the Right: Danton and his friends, who were compromised by their policy of clemency and their desire to conclude peace. Here, according to the nineteenth bulletin, sent on April 2, was how this decision, more serious than the preceding one, was taken by the Committee of Public Safety.

At the evening meeting, on the 27th, of the Committee of Public Safety, in addition to the seven members, there were also present the Abbé Sieyès and Henriot, commander of the National Guard. A resolution was passed on the motion of the Abbé Sieyès to include among the conspirators the famous Danton, who until then had been a colleague of Robespierre. The Abbé Sieyès read a memorandum of Foulquier Tainville [Fouquier-Tinville], the public prosecutor of the Revolutionary Tribunal. In this memorandum Foulquier declared that following the secret interrogation of Hébert, the latter, to obtain clemency, had admitted that Danton had been designated by Pitt as the man who should be placed at the head of affairs so that the powers could safely deal with him. These depositions of Hébert in this matter proved conclusive, but they are probably the fabrications of the Abbé Sieyès, Robespierre, and Foulquier.

Sieyès had again been the instigator. It is not impossible to suppose that Robespierre in this case too had to submit to external pressure, as he did in the trial of Hébert. Danton was his friend, and denouncing him before the Revolutionary Tribunal was an action that Robespierre would not have taken on his own.

The outcome of the trial was certain. It began on April 2. The accused, six in number, were divided into two categories. The first group, which included Danton and Desmoulins, was accused of conspiring to reestablish the monarchy and to destroy national representation and republican government. The second group, which included Fabre d'Eglantine, was accused of conspiring to slander the national state and to destroy the republican government by corruption. These were vague accusations without any proof to support them. Danton refuted them without difficulty and asked that the defense witnesses be heard. The Committee of Public Safety took fright. They obtained a decree from the Convention providing that the cases of the accused who disturbed the order were not subject to "debate." On April 5, the jury stated that it had enough facts and rendered a verdict of guilty. This provoked an uproar among the accused. The Tribunal then announced that there would be no further "arguments," and the death sentence was pronounced in the absence of the defendants, and carried out on the same day, April 5.

With the trial of Danton, the Revolution had completed its paradoxical cycle. It had begun with the Declaration of the Rights of Man and civil and political liberty and ended in totalitarian despotism by a faction controlled by a single individual. No one was left but Robespierre. He had become absolute master of all power. All opposition had been annihilated. There were no more clubs or organizations. Freedom of the press had been sacrificed. Had the problem of governing been solved?

No, it hadn't. Having exterminated his adversaries, Robespierre was more afraid than ever: decisive proof that the infernal circle of fear could not be broken except by an external force.

CHAPTER 2
Robespierre

Robespierre remains an enigma. No one has been a subject of more discussion. He was viewed with great sympathy during the first part of the nineteenth century. Later on, he was taken to be a monster. In the twentieth century there has been a return of opinion in his favor. Albert Mathiez has been his most fervent apologist. A Society for Robespierrist Studies has been established under his leadership. This admiration has grown between the two world wars to such a point that Robespierre is regarded as the authentic representative of the Revolution, its greatest and purest product. This exaggeration can be explained by the fact that Mathiez and his school have had no experience with revolutionary governments.

After the execution of Danton and his friends, Robespierre was, for several weeks, immensely popular with both the Right and the Left. Catholics and royalists counted upon him to restore order in France and to re-establish tolerable living conditions. The letters found among his papers prove this. This hope was equally shared by the courts of Vienna, Berlin, and London.

How can this popularity be explained?

For the people of the Left, Robespierre symbolized the great philosophy which culminated in the Revolution and from which stemmed the major political and social movements of the nineteenth century, socialism and communism. This doctrine is not that of the Rousseau's *Social Contract*. It goes back further, to the doctrine of natural rights vitalized in the seventeenth century by Grotius in his work *De Jure belli et pacis*. Grotius was the founder of international law. He based it on the doctrine of natural rights, which he had taken from ancient philosophy, from Stoicism and the traditional Scholasticism of Saint Thomas, but adapted to the needs of his time. It rapidly developed into a school, and its doctrine, expanded by Puffendorf, Wolf, Fénelon, Burlamaqui, Vattel, and popularized by Rousseau, was the necessary groundwork for the history of the nineteenth and twentieth centuries. Of those seven, Fénelon alone was a Catholic. The others were Protestants, four being Calvinists. It could be said that the doctrine of natural rights, personified in Robespierre, was the child of Calvinism, and that Geneva was the holy city.

The doctrine of natural rights is based on the principle

that reason enables us to know whether an act is moral or not. This power of reasoning is given to man by God. This natural right springs from a divine origin since it is an emanation of God. It is indispensable, immutable, eternal, and absolute. There are two methods of determining it: the one *a priori,* arising out of the nature of man; the other *a posteriori,* through proofs of an external nature. The first method starts from the principle that men cannot live alone, that they must live with their fellow men in an order ruled by reason. A whole series of deductions has been derived from this principle, as one can gather from the following passage from Fénelon's *Essai philosophique sur le gouvernement civil:*

We are all citizens of the universe, children of the same father . . . and as a consequence we are all born with equal rights which we need for our preservation. According to this principle, nothing is more contrary to nature than the unequal division of wealth. . . . However, if everyone were permitted to seize what he needed . . . the majority of people would use this principle to become thieves. It would be impossible to preserve order and peace, and there would be a lapse into terrible anarchy. To avoid these pitfalls, we need civil laws, such as for contracts and inheritance, to regulate the distribution of property.

We must use the same line of reasoning with regard to authority. According to natural law, which is the law of reason, he who is most capable of discovering what is just, who loves justice and will carry it out, that is to say he who is the most intelligent and virtuous, should without doubt be preferred over the less intelligent and virtuous in the distribution of authority. But since pride and love of independence and other passions bring us to prefer ourselves to others, we must find a less equivocal rule than personal qualities to determine sovereignty. This is necessary in order that society not be the continual prey of ambitions; just as it is necessary to lay down laws regulating property, so that it will not become the continuous prey of avaricious men. . . . Distinctions which are least envied are those which come from a long line of ancestors. It is for that reason that in almost all states the antiquity of families is the ruling factor.

In sum, Fénelon says that private property and hereditary power are contrary to natural rights that come directly from God. However, we must tolerate this violation to avoid the grave consequences that would result if the doctrine of natural rights were to be fully applied. Fénelon, who was a prince of the Church, lived at the height of the Old Regime. Robespierre's situation was completely different, but the ideas remained the same. He was a petty bourgeois who lived in an era in which the civil institutions of the Old Regime had lost all their usefulness. To return to the era of Fénelon was inconceivable. Robespierre, on the contrary, said that private property and hereditary power should be abolished in the name of natural rights. For Robespierre, equality was a passion. It was logical for him to demand, from the start, the abolition of the power of kings and nobles. Political equality was not enough, however. He also wanted social equality.

"A true democracy," he said, "is incompatible with inequality of wealth." Robespierre might justly be called the forefather of socialism. In one of his speeches to the Constituent Assembly he declared:

> *Great riches corrupt both those who possess them and those who desire them. In the face of great riches, virtue is disgraced, and talent itself is corrupted by luxury and is regarded less as a means of being useful to the fatherland than as the means for acquiring a fortune. Under these conditions, liberty is idle fancy and the laws are only instruments of oppression. You have done nothing for the public good if all your laws and your institutions do not aim to do away with the great inequalities of wealth. . . . Can man dispose of the land he cultivates if he is reduced to dust? No, an individual's property should return to the public domain after his death. It is not in the public interest that the first expropriator transmit his goods to his descendants. The public interest is equality.*

The ideas of Robespierre were suited to his temperament. Honest and altruistic, he was horrified by luxury; his tastes were simple and he had no need of money. In this idea of austerity we recognize the influence of Calvin as transmitted through Rousseau.

This explains the popularity of Robespierre for the men of the Left. He knew how to present the theories of natural rights with great clarity to the masses in a way that aroused them and that appealed to their secret aspirations. The men of the Right hailed him as the man who had destroyed Hébertism, and they counted upon him to govern France more wisely.

On April 5, he became the directing force, with the general consent of the Right and of the Left. All were ready to aid him in reconstructing the political and social order. Never did his position appear so strong. Two months later, on June 10 (22th Prairial), the Convention voted a law abolishing the last remaining rights of suspects. It was the worst law of the Terror—and it was to be the beginning of Robespierre's fall.

The purge of the faction of Hébert and Danton should have given new confidence to the government. But it only served to increase its fear. The victorious faction feared the discontent of the defeated parties, and they in turn lived in dread of the victorious faction. To this mutual fear was added concern with the economic situation, with unemployment, misery, and hunger. There was also great anxiety about the war. Under the impetus of England, the coalition armies prepared for a new invasion of France in the spring of 1794. Paris was restless. The Committee of Public Safety drew up plans for a counteroffensive and for the invasion of Belgium. But these were only plans. The Republic was weak and its armies were disorganized.

All this contributed to an atmosphere of general panic, and the law of Prairial only aggravated it. Till then, only the Convention had the right to denounce suspects to the Revolutionary Tribunal. With this new law, this right was extended to the Committee of Public Safety, the Committee of General Security, the Commissioners of the Convention, and the public prosecutor, Fouquier-Tinville. Nine out of ten times, the denunciation led to the death sentence. As long as the vote of the Convention had been necessary, these sentences were less frequent, as the Assembly was a slow-moving machine.

The general fear had given birth to the law of Prairial. And, of all, Robespierre was himself the most afraid. His was a justifiable fear; it is found among all heads of revolutionary governments. For a revolutionary government is, above all, tied to the person of its leader. If he disappears, the regime falls. There are two consequences of this. First, the opponents of the regime seek to kill its leader. Second, the leader defends his life not just for himself but because his death would lead to the collapse of the regime he created. A man can be asked to sacrifice his life if necessary to perpetuate his work; but you cannot ask this of a man who knows his work will perish with him.

In the two months between the death of Danton and the law of Prairial, there were two attempts to assassinate Robespierre. The second was probably only imaginary. A woman, Cécile Renaud, was suspected. The example of Charlotte Corday had not been forgotten, and Cécile Renaud was put to death. So great was the fear that sixty people—family and friends—were executed with her. Moreover, Barrère, in the name of the Committee of Public Safety, read to the Convention a report accusing the British government of having instigated this assassination plot as well as all the others, and demanded as a measure of reprisal that all British and Hanoverian prisoners be shot. The proposal was accepted. Fortunately, however, the soldiers refused to carry out the decree for fear that the same fate would be theirs if they fell into British hands. When the law collapses, heaven and earth tremble! And what unlikely extremes does this lead to!

June 10 to July 27 was a desperate time. The trials multiplied. People of all conditions and of all ages were brought to the gallows. The guillotine functioned with great efficiency. Sometimes eighty heads fell in a single day in Paris, and almost as many in the provinces.

The report of June 22 described the situation:

> It is impossible to express the fear that reigned in the Committee of Public Safety. This fear made it take the most cruel measures. The Revolutionary Tribunal, to whom the cases were blindly submitted, had 157 in eight days. The sordid population of Paris came in crowds to these executions. . . . The Municipality also denounced an uprising among workers employed in the manufacturing of assignats. The Committee, without any trial, ordered death by strangulation for fourteen of the principals, on the night of the 16th or 17th.
>
> On the morning of the 15th, notices were placed in the cafés and on the walls of Paris prohibiting, on pain of death, the "slandering" of the government or the spreading of news tending to alarm the people or to slacken their patriotic ardor. This decree was made public on the 15th, and on the 16th at four o'clock in the afternoon eleven persons were guillotined for having spread false news and having criticized the government. Matters reached such a state on the 20th that no two patriots, however prominent, could dine together three or four times without being arrested as suspects. The public prosecutor, Foulquier, in an open session of the Revolutionary Tribunal

accuses you of having laughed in such a manner; of having spoken with this or that suspected person; of having threatened the state by a gesture; if the jurors under oath say that they believe that the "charges" are true, then at four in the afternoon you go to the guillotine.

With the decree of the 22nd Prairial, the revolutionary government reached a kind of climax. It experienced an excess of morbid energy generally not known by legitimate governments. This could be seen in the progress of the war. During the summer, both sides made preparations for an offensive. The English planned to march on Paris, and the French to invade Belgium. In the spring, all the armies were on the move and the military power of the Revolution was affirmed. The French proved superior. On May 18, the Allied armies were beaten at Tourcoing; the defeat began to shake the Emperor's will to wage war. On June 13, he left for Vienna, entrusting the command to his brother, the Archduke Charles, and to the Prince of Coburg, with instructions to evacuate Belgium if the war continued to go badly. That is what happened. Jourdan, who had taken over command of the Army of the Moselle, won an important victory on June 26 at Fleurus, which led the Austrians to evacuate the Low Countries.

Could these victories offset the internal difficulties? The people lived in dread of the guillotine. A few from each side formed the nucleus of the opposition to Robespierre, for, despite his great popularity, he had made many enemies. He was accused of being a tyrant. He was reproached for his severity. Many would have preferred a spendthrift, indeed a corrupt government, to a puritanical one. Robespierre's deism had gained him enemies too. He had established the cult of the Supreme Being. Since his inauguration on the 20th Prairial, he had become a kind of grand pontiff—which was displeasing not only to Catholics but to nonbelievers and libertines as well. Finally, Robespierre had formidable adversaries in the small group of terrorists who felt threatened by him.

If he supported the law of the 22nd Prairial, it was with the prospect of a new purge, the last, he thought. He wished to eliminate seven or eight members who were hated because of their acts of terror or because of their scandalous behavior. Among them were Fouché, responsible for the shootings at Lyons; Carrier, for the judicial drownings at Nantes; Barras and Tallien, for the massacres at Marseilles and Bordeaux. This law, intended as the final purge, became instead the instrument of revenge. During this surge of terrorist ferocity, Robespierre bided his time. He did nothing, or almost nothing. He did not want to repeal the law of Prairial (which would be used to purge him), but neither did he make use of it. Instead, he waited for a favorable opportunity—which never presented itself, as his enemies were protected by the Convention and the Committee of Public Safety. Finally, he broke with the Committee and stopped attending meetings. He was completely isolated. If he could have been identified with the Terror, it would have been easier to overthrow him. That is what his enemies tried to do. But it was not easy. He had introduced the law of Prairial, but he was not responsible for its savage application.

Not inclined to allow itself to be sacrificed to the ideal of virtue, the terrorist group, threatened by Robespierre, secretly began to work on the Convention and its moderate majority, which since the establishment of the completely revolutionary government no longer attended the sessions. This majority sought to organize a more humane government. The conscience of France responded to their efforts, which called forth a strong response. The meetings of the Convention were better attended. The origins of this movement are, without doubt, somewhat contradictory. The worst of the terrorists formed the vanguard of the reaction against the Terror, which in the end became personified in Robespierre.

This political maneuver had its first results. On July 25 (7th Thermidor), Barrère presented a report to the Convention, in the name of the Committee of Public Safety, censuring those to whom the victories were not reassuring and who were planning new proscriptions. The improvement in the military situation operated in favor of a more reasonable political program. It was evident that the war, without being the cause of the Terror, had facilitated its operation, and now a change was justified. A revolutionary government never says to its subjects, "I am oppressing you because I fear you." It always finds another excuse, for example, the necessity to defend the Revolution against its enemies or to protect it against the counterrevolution. However, the cry against counterrevolution did not rally everyone. The royalists, who were in a majority, wanted the counterrevolution. When a revolutionary government can justify its terrorist measures in the name of national security, it has unanimous support behind it, since everyone, more or less, now consents to great sacrifices. But the improvement of the military situation in June 1794 removed a great deal of the force of the argument that the terrorist measures were dictated by the dangers facing the nation. The danger of invasion having been removed, let us return, it was being said, to more reasonable methods of government. Also, Barrère's report created a sensation, and the Convention voted that it be printed.

On the next day, the 8th Thermidor, Robespierre replied in a speech in which he protested against the accusation of dictatorship and terrorism. It was a passionate attack on criminals and those guilty of corruption, who should be, he said, ousted from the Convention and its committees. When asked for names, Robespierre was careful not to give them. "Then the Convention must itself decide," exclaimed one deputy. On the night of the 8th to the 9th Thermidor, the small terrorist group attacked by Robespierre redoubled its efforts to bring the moderate elements to the following day's session of the Convention. On the tenth, Tallien and Billaud-Varennes finally dared to accuse Robespierre openly in the name of humanity and legality. This attack was successful. The majority recovered its courage. Robespierre tried to reply, but he was not able to make himself heard above the uproar. Robespierre, Saint-Just, and Couthon, the three most prominent members of the government, were arrested. The arrest and replacement of Hanriot, the head of the National Guard, were also ordered. This last was illegal since the Guard was responsible to the Paris Commune. Which of the two was the real head: Hanriot or his replacement? Robespierre and his colleagues were freed by Hanriot, who escorted them to the Municipality, summoned the National Guard, and made preparations for resistance at the Hôtel de Ville.

Two powers confronted each other: the Convention and the Commune. The former, signally weak, possessed no armed force, but in a burst of energy it outlawed Robespierre and his friends. A terrible decree, since no trial was needed to send them to the gallows. To impose its will upon the Commune, it appealed to the National Guard to arm and place itself under the command of Barras. This was illegal, but the revolutionary measure was completely successful.

At the time when the Commune was dominated by the supporters of Hébert, the majority of the National Guard, who belonged to the upper classes, had not responded to the call, so as not to become the instrument of a political policy to which they were opposed. This abstention did not arouse any protest. It helped the extremist party, which was less numerous but more united. This time the summons was issued by the Convention, and the bourgeois elements hastened to answer. There were now two national guards: a proletarian national guard in the service of the Commune, and a bourgeois national guard serving the Convention and under the orders of Barras. The encounter was less violent than might have been expected. It was Robespierre himself who did not wish to push matters to an extreme. He proved thus that he was not only a revolutionary but also a statesman. He understood that a victory over the Convention would be suicidal, for the Convention was the only institution that still possessed a semblance of legality. It was due to this semblance of legality that for a short while after the fall of Robespierre a certain degree of order was reestablished which gave France a respite. What state would France have been in if Robespierre had overthrown the Convention? The government would have been able to keep itself in power only by an ever greater abuse of power. Hence, he renounced the struggle. On the night of the ninth to the tenth, Barras marched on the Hôtel de Ville. Robespierre and his friends were taken and were executed on the following day. Thus the first totalitarian revolutionary government, the Terror, came to an end. It had lasted from June 2, 1793, to July 27, 1794.

What is the judgment on Robespierre? The historians of the Right and of the Left have pronounced very different verdicts.

Taine, in his *Origins of Contemporary France*, says:

The Revolution demands another interpreter, like itself with a false veneer, and such is Robespierre, with his irreproachable appearance, his hair well powdered, his clothes carefully brushed, his manners correct, his tone dogmatic, his style studied and dull. No other mind, by its mediocrity and its shortcomings, was so congenial to the spirit of the times. He was the antithesis of a statesman, he hovered in a void, amid abstractions, always standing on principles and incapable of stepping down to a practical footing. "That b—— there," said Danton, "does not even know how to boil an egg." Another contemporary wrote: "The vague generalities of his preaching usually did not result in any measure or law. He opposed everything and proposed nothing. The lack of policy was in accord with his intellectual impotence and lack of legislative concepts. When he unwound the thread of his revolutionary scholasticism, he was finished. In matters of finance or of the art of the military he knew nothing, and risked nothing, save to denigrate and slander Carnot and Cambon, who did know and who did take risks. With respect to foreign policy, his speech on the state of Europe was the explanation of a schoolboy. When he exposed the plans of the English ministry, he reached the height of fantastic foolishness. These are not the words of a head of government but of a porter at the Jacobin club. He lacked any ideas about contemporary France, the real France as it actually was. In place of people he saw twenty-six million automatons to be molded so that they might function harmoniously. Indeed, since they were naturally good, after a small but necessary purification all would be well again, since the collective will is 'the voice of reason and the public interest.' That is why they are wise when they are together. 'If possible, the assembly of the delegates of the people should deliberate in the presence of all the people'; at least the legislative body should meet 'in a vast and majestic edifice open to twelve thousand spectators.'" It should be noted that at the Constituent Assembly, at the Legislative Assembly, in the Convention, at the Hôtel de Ville, and in the Jacobin club—wherever Robespierre was to be found, the galleries never ceased to raise a hubbub. The shock of such a positive, palpable experience would affect any mind; his remained closed either through prejudice or through interest. Truth, even physical facts, could not enter his mind because he was unable to comprehend it or needed to exclude it. He was, then, obtuse or a charlatan. In fact, he was both, because the two combine to form a vulgar, pedantic individual, one who, having a hollow, inflated mind, believes, because it is filled with words, that he is full of ideas and revels in his own phrases. It dupes itself that it may dictate to others.

And this is what Albert Mathiez said about Robespierre in a lecture published in Paris under the title "Pourquoi nous sommes robespierristes?" ("Why are we Robespierrists?"):

We love Robespierre because he understood and practiced the art of government, aptly described in our times as sacerdotal. "In politics," Robespierre said, "nothing is just unless it is honest, nothing is useful unless it is just" (May 9, 1791). He wanted politics to be moral. Evidently the people of the fraternal Republic failed to understand.

We love Robespierre because he did not fear to attack the vulgar prejudices when it was necessary. We love him because he never feared ridicule, because he repeated tirelessly a truth which he had taken from Jean-Jacques Rousseau and Montesquieu, that of all forms of government democracy was the most difficult to practice since it requires a devotion to the

*public good, also known as virtue. He practiced what he
preached....*

*We love Robespierre because he was the incarnation of all
that was most noble, generous, and sincere. We love him for
the lessons of his life and the symbol of his death. He succumbed to the blows of rogues. The legend, cunningly forged
by his enemies, who are the enemies of social progress, has
even misled republicans, who do not understand him and
would bless him as a saint if they did. These injustices endear
him to us even more.*

*We love Robespierre because his name, vilified by those
whom he wanted to set free, summarizes all the social iniqui-
ties which we want to have disappear. In consecrating ourselves to rehabilitating his memory, we are not only serving
historical truth; we know for certain that we are doing something important for France, which must become what she was
at the time of Robespierre, the champion of justice, the hope
of the oppressed, the terror of the oppressors, the torch of the
universe.*

*Robespierre and his followers were great men because they
understood that governmental action, no matter how resolute,
would be powerless to galvanize the energy of the French
people if it were not directly associated with the execution of
the laws, with a clear and confident policy. It is time that
statesmen who are entrusted with the formidable task of heal-
ing the nation's wounds be inspired by their example.*

Two distinguished personalities from the same country,
from the same background and nurtured by the same
culture, reached diametrically opposite views on so noted
a figure as Robespierre. This dualism is frightening be-

cause of its enormous consequences to Western civilization. It must be explained some day when the true history of the Revolution is written.

Let us try to discover the weaknesses of the two judgments. Taine's is beside the point. His is less a judgment of Robespierre than an indirect attack on the doctrine of natural rights. For Robespierre, it was a religious truth from which he drew all his strength. During the nineteenth century, the doctrine of natural rights was attacked by the positivist school, to which Taine belonged, as a metaphysical doctrine outside of reality and not appropriate to politics. Taine displayed a twofold antipathy, as a conservative and as a positivist. But he was in error. The doctrine of natural rights was one of the great forces of history since the beginning of the nineteenth century, because it expressed real passions and moral imperatives: of bringing humanity and equality to the society of the Old Regime. One may not approve of it, but one cannot deny that it was a truly effective force. Taine's censure of Robespierre is in reality a censure of natural rights. Such a judgment is not just.

Mathiez is closer to the truth when he says that Robespierre represented what was essential in the Revolution. Mathiez was also right in trying to refute the legend of a Robespierre thirsting for blood. That is obviously an exaggeration. There were two kinds of revolutionary: Robespierre's and Napoleon's. To the first kind belong men who are attached to an idea, which they believe in religiously and which makes them unwilling to compromise regardless of the cost. To the second belong those who have no ideals of their own but who toy with all ideas. The weak point in Mathiez's argument is his conclusion:

I do not know if I have convinced you, but I can at least say without reservation what we are and what we want. We believe that since 1908 our society has served courageously and impartially not just the cause of one man, not even the cause of a party, but the cause of France, of contemporary France, which remains loyal to its traditions. We believe that the efforts of our society, which has struggled, without losing courage, against indifference, ignorance, disdain, and hostility, have not been in vain either in the realm of science or in that of actions. We are proud that it has indirectly prepared for the moral crisis which the war helped to bring about and which will end by purifying the atmosphere in which presently our free institutions run the risk of withering and dying. We believe that our independent researches, our struggle for ideas, are preparing a future for this new republic, a future desired by so many. We hope that from the very depths, which we are so close to, will finally surge forth an organized, living democracy, invincible because it will be just and fraternal; the city of equality for which Robespierre and Saint-Just died; the city of liberty for which millions of unknown heroes have spilled their blood.

There are the reasons, ladies and gentlemen, why we proclaim ourselves Robespierrists.

To offer Robespierre as a model is to be completely without a sense of historical reality. It was not by such a government that France was inspired in 1920. France, having been the first to experiment with a revolutionary government, knew better than any other how frightful it was.

CHAPTER 3
The Thermidorian Reaction

On the 9th Thermidor, the revolutionary government was overthrown because an external force broke the infernal circle of fear and the abuse of power that had held it prisoner. The force was the moderate majority of the Convention. It should always have been the dominant authority, but the revolutionary government had paralyzed it. Finally becoming conscious of its duties, it reasserted itself and carried the Parisian bourgeoisie with it. This left its imprint on the reaction that followed, which is known in history as the Thermidorian reaction. It was a general reaction against the government of the Terror, which had suppressed all liberties. There was an

203

endeavor, to a certain degree at least, to reestablish these liberties. Debates were resumed in the Convention. The right of opposition was recognized, and the government rapidly restored parliamentary procedures. The Committees of Public Safety and General Security were reorganized by the Convention, and their prerogatives limited. They were placed under the close supervision of the Convention. The National Guard was purged of its most revolutionary elements, and henceforth the Convention could count on its support. The extremists were expelled from the Jacobins. All the decrees dealing with the economy were revoked. The religious policies were radically modified. In February 1795, the Convention proclaimed religious freedom for all, warning that it would prosecute anyone who opposed this right. The churches were returned both to juring and non-juring priests. Attendance was greater than ever.

What is the significance of this reaction? It was an attempt to escape from the second revolution and return to the first, that of the Rights of Man and parliamentary government. This effort was manifested above all in the constitution of the year III, which was the principal work of the Thermidorian reaction. The constitution of 1793 had never been put into force. A product of fear, it was an extremist constitution which had followed the democratic orientation of the state, adopting universal suffrage. The constitution of the Convention, which was drafted after the fall of Robespierre and was in effect until the 18th Brumaire, was more moderate and practical, having been drawn up in a period of relative confidence. It no longer rested upon the principle of universal suffrage. In order to be an elector, it was necessary to pay a small tax. The system of election by two degrees, abolished by the constitution of 1793, was reestablished: the active citizens chose electors, who in turn chose the deputies. It was a return to a system of suffrage based on property, but with an expanded electorate. However, in order to qualify as an elector of the second degree, it was necessary to possess considerable wealth.

Legislative power was conferred upon two elected chambers: the Council of Ancients, numbering 250 members; and the Council of Five Hundred. One-third of each house was to be elected each year. The constitution of the year III was the first constitution of the Revolution which divided the legislative assembly into two bodies. This division, which followed the examples of the English and American constitutions, was wise. The powers were not equally divided between the two councils. There was a desire to prevent a proliferation of laws, which had been produced too easily under the Terror. The power to initiate laws belonged exclusively to the Council of Five Hundred. When approved by that body, they were called resolutions; then, if approved by the Ancients, they became laws. Those resolutions which were rejected by the Ancients could not be proposed again for at least a year.

This constitution displayed a certain mistrust of youth. Members of the Five Hundred had to be at least thirty years old; members of the Council of Ancients had to be at least forty and either married or widowed. Revolutionary governments generally look favorably upon youth; legitimate governments, on the contrary, tend toward government by older people. Civilized societies can only be governed by men of maturity. Youth has great *élan* but is too easily frightened.

The organization of the executive power was partly inspired by the American constitution. It was independent of the legislative power. Instead of being delegated to a single president, it was given to a Directory of five members, all aged forty or over, elected by the legislative body. The Council of Five Hundred drew up a secret list containing ten times as many names as there would be directors, from which the Council of Ancients made the selection by secret ballot. One director was replaced each year. Ministers, who were chosen by the Directory, were not subject to the control of the legislative bodies. Here we see the American influence and a dislike of the British parliamentary system. The ministers simply acted as secretaries to the Directory and had no communication with the legislature. Assisted by the ministers, the directors were in charge of all affairs. They could propose a declaration of war, but the legislature alone could declare war. The directors negotiated treaties, but they had to be ratified by the legislature.

These formal and complicated constitutional provisions were a crown of ice encrusted on an easily recognized volcano of passions: the horror of dictatorship, the fear of mixing legislative and executive powers, and the mistrust of universal suffrage. Despite the complications which masked so much distrust, the constitution prepared by the Thermidorians was sufficiently broad, free, and wise to have satisfied France—if it could have been acted upon. Without achieving universal suffrage, the constitution recognized the citizenship of the great majority, since those who owned nothing and paid no taxes could not have been very numerous. The two-stage elections and the limited franchise for electors of the second degree did not constitute such an unjust privilege that it would seem intolerable in a country that had scarcely had the experience of representative government, a country, moreover, in which the aristocratic traditions were still so strong.

Along with freedom of the press, the constitution of the year III guaranteed everyone the right to speak up. The general will, the new source of legitimate power, could now be made known and assert itself. This was the principal task of the Revolution. Besides, the executive power was so strong and so clearly separated from legislative power that the continual encroachment of the Convention was no longer to be feared. The constitution of the year III, could it have been carried out, would have brought to a happy conclusion the stormy period of the Revolution.

What fatality destined the Revolution to violate its principles continually without ever renouncing them! The knot which strangled it was loosened for a moment and then was tightened again. During Thermidor, the Convention succeeded in reestablishing legality, in guaranteeing order and a degree of political, religious, and economic liberty. This liberty led to the revival of all those latent forces that the Jacobin dictatorship had harshly repressed: not only Catholicism, but what was more serious for the Thermidorians, royalism as well. Since the beginning of 1795, there had been quite a strong revival of the monarchical tradition. In more than one section of Paris, the National Guard and groups of youths openly declared themselves royalists. The salons became more and more disrespectful of the Republic and the Revolution; the use of "thee" and "thou" ceased, and the red hats of the Revolution were proscribed. What was worse, the victims of yesterday began to apply the rule of retribution against their former oppressors, and the government lacked the power to enforce a respect for law. The term "terrorist" in many regions of France became a cause for banishment, as that of "aristocrat" had been under the Terror. The reaction was most terrible in the Midi.

All this was inevitable. The monarchical tradition was too strong in France to disappear suddenly. Royalty had only succumbed to an unforeseen juncture of circumstances because of the hostility of the masses. Once the Terror was over, it was natural that a yearning for the return of time-honored institutions would take hold and spread throughout the population. Also, the overthrow of the monarch had been followed by the most terrible calamities: war, famine, misery, tyranny, terror, massacres. The monarchy seemed a regime of peace, prosperity, and happiness.

Now France was governed by an aristocracy of regicides, as they were termed. It was natural too that at the moment when they were prepared to grant the constitution of the year III they were seized once again by fear. This resulted once again in violence, though this time in another form. What could be expected from elections that took place in the midst of general restlessness, both on the part of the royalists and on that of the anti-revolutionaries?

And what if the people whom the Revolution had consecrated as sovereign were to use this sovereignty to oppose the Revolution? The aristocracy of regicides had no illusions. Though the enemies and victims of the Revolution had aided the regicides during the bloody despotism of the Jacobins, on the day when these anti-revolutionaries in turn became masters of the state, they would not forgive the regicides for their vote against the king, or for all the crimes and violence which the Convention had assented to, willingly or not. Almost all the Thermidorians had been at least passive accomplices of the Terror. On the day that the victims demanded an accounting, the argument that the Terror had been made necessary by fear would not be a good enough excuse. The aristocracy of regicides consisted of men too shrewd not to ask themselves whether the constitution of the year III would not be the suicide of the Revolution, which was serious, or their own suicide, which was even more serious.

The new constitution was in theory a good one. Its operation, however, required the wholehearted cooperation of the majority of the middle and upper classes.

There was no such cooperation, however, because after 9th Thermidor a disagreement arose between the royalists and the republicans over the decree of January 1795 proclaiming the anniversary of the execution of Louis XVI a national holiday. To the royalists, the decree was a slap in the face. The decree was in fact the response of the Convention to those who held that the execution was an inexpiable crime and who accused the Convention of regicide. At this time the punishment for such a crime was most severe.

The members of the Convention were regicides, yes, but out of necessity. The moderate majority had voted for the death penalty against its will, under the pressure of Jacobin extremism and of the armed bands in the service of the Mountain. But they did vote it, and the act was too serious to be forgotten or disavowed. Unable to forget or disavow it, the Convention treated it as a meritorious act of civic heroism. The decree of January excluded henceforth any possibility of agreement between the royalists and the moderates.

The moderate majority of the Convention thus took an intermediate position, characterized by the condemnation of terrorism on the one hand, and the glorification of the execution of Louis XVI on the other. Not to have incurred any responsibility for the Terror but to have voted for the death of the king were the two prerequisites for becoming an influential member of the group that directed the state. This was a difficult position. Those who were compromised, in one way or another, under the Terror, and those who clung to the monarchy, together constituted a majority in the country. Together, the extreme Right and the extreme Left could form a coalition from one day to the next, a paradoxical and transitory coalition to be sure, but one which could not fail to create serious difficulties for the party that governed the Republic.

In the course of that year, 1795, something else occurred which increased the fear of the Thermidorian government. On June 8, the most pathetic victim of the Terror, the son of Louis XVI, for the royalists Louis XVII, the legitimate sovereign of France, died at the Temple. This poor sick infant lived in a dungeon. His existence obsessed the party in power, since they believed that he was a permanent menace to them. As long as the Dauphin lived, England would seek to reestablish the monarchy in his person. If he died, the restoration could not take place, because the powers, and primarily England, would never allow one who was capable of ruling, such as the future Louis XVIII, to mount the throne of the Bourbons. The infant, for whom a regency would have to be established, would have assured a government sufficiently stable so that France would no longer constitute a danger to Europe and sufficiently weak so that it would no longer be a constant concern. The revolutionary party wanted to rid itself of the Dauphin, and since it could not guillotine him, it sought to hasten his death by ill treatment. To satisfy the public conscience and the royalists, the Thermidorians had him looked after, but they continued to hold him prisoner, for to them also he was a great embarrassment.

There was general relief when the infant died: the

delusion was that the monarchy had been eliminated forever. The child's death, on the contrary, reinforced the position of the royalists in an unexpected way. An unfortunate infant, held hostage in the dungeons of the Revolution, powerless despite his title of sovereign, was succeeded by an able individual, Louis XVIII, the only truly intelligent member of the family, who, despite his exile, had a choice of several courses of action. It was he who resolved the problem raised but not answered by the Revolution, that of the right of opposition. In 1795, no one imagined that the Count of Provence, who was wandering over Europe from one course to another, would one day play an extraordinary role.

When royalist enthusiasm revived in France and became aggressive, it served only to increase the dominant party's concern regarding the application of the new constitution. Fear, checked for a moment by the revival of courage, now took hold of the Thermidorian government, just as it had in the preceding one. This fear could only become greater in the months to come. The first effect was the creation of a home force for the defense of the Convention.

The military force charged with maintaining order in Paris and defending the Assembly was the National Guard. After the 9th Thermidor, the more revolutionary political elements were expelled and the bourgeois elements reinforced. However, as a result of the disagreement between the royalists and the Convention, the Convention no longer had confidence in the National Guard. The

National Guard had been too extremist; now it was too Catholic and too royalist. A home force of five thousand men was organized, recruited from army deserters who had taken refuge in Paris: a sort of praetorian guard for a new collective monarchy.

The new constitution was to be ratified by the nation. It was submitted to primary assemblies: homage rendered to the democratic principle of national sovereignty. Two extraordinary provisions were added to it—those of August 22 and August 30, 1795, which were also to be submitted for popular approval—stating that two-thirds of the members of the Convention were to become part of the new legislative bodies. The Convention reserved 500 of the 750 seats in the subsequent assemblies for itself. The aristocracy of regicides thus assured itself of a majority in the new legislature. At the moment that it placed the royal crown on its own head, it tied the hands of the people, out of fear that in a free election they might vote for the royalists.

After having vanquished the revolutionary government of the Terror, the Thermidorians had attempted to constitute a regular representative government. This effort, if not completely successful, had satisfactory results. And now these two decrees which would compromise everything! Only a minority of Frenchmen, however, recognized the Thermidorian government. It was not sufficiently legitimate that it could entrust itself to the intelligent free will of the people. Driven by fear, it allowed itself to violate the very principles of the Revolution over which it had proclaimed itself guardian. France was once again on the slippery slope to revolutionary government.

Legitimacy confers power. It determines who shall have the right to command and who shall have the duty to obey. It is not necessarily rational. Sometimes, indeed, it is absurd. Such, for example, is the case with the hereditary principle. What is the guarantee that the beneficiary of this principle would possess the qualities to exercise power? But, once accepted, the principle of legitimacy becomes a serious matter, indeed sacred. It must be, with all its shortcomings, loyally accepted; otherwise, society is plunged into terrible chaos.

The Thermidorians had wanted to establish a representative government by accepting the principle of popular sovereignty: power is legitimate when it is delegated by the people. This principle is valid only if the power is granted freely. If it is imposed upon the people by the government, the principle of legitimacy is transformed into a parody and the government cannot be legitimate. The constitution of the year III established the sovereignty of the people. What became of this sovereignty as a result of the "two-thirds" decrees?

Today's chaos is the result of a similar situation. Two-thirds of Europe is governed by states that pretend to rest on the principle of national sovereignty but in reality use it as did the Convention: power, instead of being delegated by the people, obliges them to yield it up.

The "two-thirds" decrees provoked great excitement in Paris. The center, the rich, the most substantial party in

the National Guard, the bourgeoisie who had been responsible for the ferment of '89, the gilded youth, almost all
elements that aided the Thermidorians in overthrowing
the Jacobins and the Terror turned against the Convention. They accused it of tyranny and invoked the principles of the Revolution against it.

On the 1st Vendémiaire (September 23), the Convention made public the results of the plebiscite on the constitutional laws. The results were disastrous because of the
ridiculously small number of voters. Out of an electoral
body of five million, the constitution of the year III did
not even get a million votes, whereas the constitution of
1793 had received two million votes. The number of abstentions was enormous. Only 263,000 voters cast their ballots
during August, and a third of them had the courage to
vote against the laws. These figures indicated how isolated
the Convention was throughout the country. It represented only a minority of France.

For a moment it seemed possible that these decrees
would be revoked. But nothing was done; after the plebiscite, the Convention was more determined than ever to
enforce these laws. The coalition of moderate republicans
and royalists that had led the campaign of opposition did
not hesitate, in its turn, to resort to force. It controlled the
National Guard in Paris. The Convention entrusted
Barras with its defense. The clash occurred on the 13th
Vendémiaire. When the National Guard attempted to
attack the Convention, it was greeted with an artillery
barrage that it was unable to overcome.

The 13th Vendémiaire is celebrated in history as having

made Napoleon's fortune. Tradition has it that it was he who saved the Convention by crushing the attack of the National Guard. This version originated in the letters Napoleon wrote to one of his brothers, but it has been denied by Barras. In his memoirs, Barras reduces the role played by Napoleon to a minor one and claims that Napoleon disappeared at the most critical moment. Which of the two versions is correct? It is difficult to say. The official reports of the Convention appear to support Barras. We might have here an attempt at a hoax. Napoleon's career was marked by gigantic strides in the art of journalistic fraud. Napoleon well understood this new strategy, and he perfected it to an extraordinary degree.

On the other hand, it is accepted dogma among all historians that Napoleon saved the Revolution from its excesses. Taken literally, nothing is further from the truth. It must not be forgotten that there were two revolutions: that of the Rights of Man, and that of revolutionary despotism, which led to the constitution of the year VIII and the establishment of a totalitarian state. Napoleon began his career by opposing those who wanted to restore the great tradition of '89 and establish a representative state in France.

Thus, the celebrated decrees became law. Seven days later, the legislative elections began. The electoral assemblies met from October 12 to October 21. However, so great was the opposition to the decrees that only 379 Convention members were reelected, instead of 500. Those reelected met in an electoral assembly and proceeded to make a quorum. On October 26, the Convention dissolved.

The following is Albert Sorel's appraisal of the Convention:

The Convention went from one extreme to the other. It surprised the world by its military audacity, swept France along, made Europe tremble, and imposed peace upon kings. It degraded itself under the tyrannical rule of several bloody fanatics; it did not know how to govern itself or how to guard its independence against the armed rabble of Paris. It claimed to have inaugurated the reign of pure reason but constantly bowed to reasons of state. It proclaimed abstract rights only to deceive the people. It achieved the most sublime as well as the most abominable and absurd goals. Its name is linked with the memory of the defense of the nation as well as with the Terror. It passed, almost without debate, great social laws which promised a great future, and yet it wasted innumerable sessions discussing arbitrary expedients, personalities, immediate needs, utopias, decrees of proscription and of persecution. It put the stamp of national unity on France but was itself consumed by factions. It gave France some of the most illustrious dates of its history and some of the most shameful. It brought forward such heroes as Desaix, Marceau, and Hoche, as well as scoundrels like Carrier. Never had France appeared so magnificent from the outside and so sordid from the inside as under this government. Made up largely of men from the legal profession, it excelled only in warfare; chosen to establish liberty in France, it prepared the way for dictatorship by an army commander. It claimed to establish a basis for an eternal peace, to set for France those limits set by nature itself, to spread fraternity among the people of the Old World: instead, the fatal consequences of these principles were the unleashing of a terrible conflict between France and her neighbors. It set off a general revolt of the people against kings; yet its politics led France into agreement with kings to divide territories and nations. Its actions were stupendous; its contradictions confusing; its sudden changes disconcerting. One would not be able to pass any final judgment upon what it did if, throughout its aberrations, it had not remained faithful to two objectives that constituted its raison d'être, *its unity, and its historic grandeur. These objectives were to preserve the national independence of France and to guarantee the rights which the French people had gained by the Revolution.*

A keen judgment, indeed! But what is the underlying cause of such a singular fate? How was it possible? How could the Convention during the first three years have been responsible for such terrible contradictions if they had not been born of an inevitable necessity stronger than the intelligence and will of men? Sorel poses the question. Here is his answer:

At the heart of all these paradoxes and sophisms which misled the Convention, we discover the terrible principle of unanimity. All groups desire it, all groups believe it necessary, but each one imagines it according to its own picture of utopia or its own purpose or goals, and it is this notion of the necessary unity of doctrine and political power which engenders the most intense conflict. For want of power to convince by discussion, each strives to exclude and oppress the other.

218

The desire for unanimity led the Convention to commit many acts of violence and many errors. Each faction that seized power thought only of eliminating its adversaries in order to achieve unanimity. Can we be satisfied with this explanation and simply maintain that the Convention was prey to a dangerous passion for unanimity? Of all its contradictions, its desire for unanimity was the most serious and the most contrary to its very nature. This assembly which should have been the sovereign power of a representative government should not have sought unanimity. There should have been discussion at the Convention. The opposition should have been able to make its views known. In representative governments, the political forces are divided into the majority and the minority. The majority has the right to rule. The minority has the right to constitute the opposition and to attempt, in turn, to become the majority by convincing the sovereign, that is, the people, that the affairs of state would be in better hands if they were in power. The Convention, however, would not tolerate any opposition. They denied the very essence of the government they claimed to represent. But why had the Revolution proclaimed those principles which it could neither disavow nor carry out?

The reason is always the same. The Convention was an illegitimate government. Right from its election, it represented only a small minority of France. This in itself was serious, and when combined with the general anarchy, it became even worse. There was no public force capable of maintaining order. The National Guard could not provide even for the physical safety of the Convention, which was forced to submit to the pressure of the turbulent bands recruited from the masses. The Mountain was thus able to force the Assembly, over the opposition of a majority, to pass the death sentence against the king. From the beginning, a minority imposed its will over the majority, contrary to the very spirit of the institution. Overcome with fear, the minority saw plots and conspiracies everywhere and would not tolerate opposition. After the elimination of the Girondists, the three groups in power, the Robespierrists, the Dantonists, and the Hébertists, ended by destroying each other. That is why the postulate of unanimity dominated the entire history of the Convention. It is to the Convention that one must look for the causes and contradictions, and not to the republican institutions, which are capable of functioning in a perfectly normal fashion. The principles of representative government do not inevitably carry with them ruinous consequences. The Swiss example since 1848 is proof of this. It was because it proclaimed principles that it was unable to carry out that the Convention led a stormy existence.

The Directory marked the decisive struggle between the first and the second revolutions. After having made a sincere effort to carry out the constitution of the year III, the Directory was faced with ever-mounting difficulties which brought about its downfall and led to the constitution of the year VIII. This, in turn, consecrated the victory of the second revolution.

The French Revolution raises another fundamental problem: that of military effectiveness. When the Revolution broke out, the neighboring monarchies feared the contagion of its example. But they also manifested a certain complaisance toward the Revolution, being persuaded that it had weakened France as a military power. This was a grievous error. After several disastrous experiences, the Revolution displayed enormous military might, far superior to the Old Regime. In the period preceding the 9th Thermidor, the French achieved great military success. On the very day on which Robespierre was overthrown in Paris, Jourdan entered Liége and forced the coalition to evacuate Belgium. On August 9, the Army of the Rhine occupied Trèves and forced the Prussians to withdraw toward Mainz. There was then a pause, not altogether unrelated to the political upheaval in Paris. But at the beginning of September, the French resumed the offensive. Holland was attacked. The English suffered a defeat and retreated to the right bank of the Meuse. Nijmegen surrendered on November 3. The Austrians were thrown back to the Rhine. On November 4, Jourdan entered Cologne, and the following day Maëstricht capitulated. In one year, the Republic had been able to conquer territories which the monarchy had coveted for centuries. As a result of these successes, the King of Prussia began negotiations with France on December 8. It was the first time that an adversary of the Revolution had sued for peace. At this moment, Holland also fell to France. This conquest alone would have justified the formation of a coalition against France for having destroyed the balance of power of the Continent. Had not the invasion of Holland a century earlier brought about a coalition of almost all of Europe against Louis XIV? This time, however, the coalition broke up. Had the Revolution become so powerful within two years that it could impose itself on all of Europe?

Yet the French armies, lacking money, found themselves in extreme want. They lacked horses, ammunition, and stores. The soldiers were half naked. Even the generals were without some of the most indispensable articles. In the occupied countries, the troops were better off. But their supplies were defective and insufficient. Jourdan lacked the pontoons necessary for crossing the Rhine, and horses for his artillery and his baggage. At Mainz, Kléber did not have a quarter of the cannons or provisions necessary to undertake the siege of the city. Now that the danger of invasion had been removed, many soldiers returned home, prompted by the terrible conditions. The government was unable to recall them to a sense of duty. The levy of '93 had not specified the length of service, and the soldiers took advantage of this to reduce it at will. Many of them took refuge in Paris, and, for want of something better, the Convention formed them into battalions for its own defense.

When it became known that deserters were not being prosecuted, the desertions multiplied so rapidly that from the middle of 1794 to the middle of 1795 the armies lost half of their effective forces. Under these conditions, how was it that the French armies inspired such fear in Europe and continued to achieve success? How was the political anarchy of the Revolution transmuted into such a powerful military force?

War is an art like any other. It has its own instruments and follows its own particular goals. It may be pursued by different methods. Each era has its own method of making war which is crystallized in its military organization, the instruction of officers, the strategy of its generals, and the principles of its diplomats. These are the same for all states. However, if at a given moment one of the combatants changes his methods, everything is put in doubt. There follows a crisis in the military relations between that state and those which still hold to the old ways but which, conscious of their inferiority, see themselves obliged to adopt new ones. This is not always a simple matter. Such a turn of events occurred in a violent and unexpected fashion during the Revolution. The rules of the game were abruptly changed.

The wars of the Old Regime presented two essential characteristics. The states had limited means, since they had few men and little money—there was no conscription and soldiers were expensive—and they pursued fixed goals. These were wars of aggrandizement and equilibrium, governed by certain rules which permitted the governments to arrive as rapidly as possible, and with a minimum of sacrifice, at their set goals. These rules were aimed at making the military more certain and less expensive, and at reducing the risks of war—that explosive

223

force which has always threatened to carry states to dangerous extremes. Under Louis XIV, one of these rules was the creation of supply facilities at the rear lines of the armies, to prevent the "nourishment of war by war," that is, to prevent the troops from living off the land by pillaging the occupied territories.

With the Revolution, the means for waging war multiplied and the goals became more vague. The goal at the beginning was the liberation of peoples; then it became the attainment of natural boundaries. This quickly led to a disruption of the balance of power in Europe which all the wars of the seventeenth and eighteenth centuries had sought to maintain. The methods also changed. There was no longer a need to economize with soldiers, and the strategy no longer consisted of avoiding battles. Under the Old Regime, there was no thought of destroying the enemy army; such destruction required great sacrifices. There was only the attempt to place the adversary in such a position as to force him to concede precisely that for which the war was being waged. Most often, this involved the cession of territory, and negotiations were carried on throughout the fighting. All this was changed by the Revolution, for the officers were no longer noblemen, as before. These were new men who ignored all the rules of the Old Regime and made war in whatever manner seemed most expeditious. They sought immediate advantages, for the Revolution needed successes. They were eager for battle and did not spare the lives of their soldiers. When they were victorious, they shunned all possibilities of concluding a peace. The great tragedy of the Revolution was its inability to make peace.

Conscription permitted the Revolution to adopt a new method of warfare that placed the adversary in a most difficult situation. It is here that one must look for the causes of all the French victories, and not in the personal qualities of Napoleon. He was clearly a great general. However, if he was victorious in so many battles, it was because of the powerful instrument forged by the Directory, which he had in his hands. Until 1814, the history of the Revolution consisted only of the intensive exploitation of its military superiority. This great power would disrupt the equilibrium of the continental forces and create a universal monarchy of which the European powers wanted no part.

This is the key to more recent events. The military power of totalitarian regimes in Europe depends upon their revolutionary situation. It is no longer superiority in numbers that assures their position, as conscription has become universal; it is superiority in expenditures. A revolutionary state is free to spend considerable sums for its armaments, whereas legitimate democracies, which must account for their expenditures, cannot exceed certain limits.

The military superiority of the Revolution was confirmed by successive stages under the Directory. The Italian campaign was its first great undertaking. It had important consequences, as it marked a decisive turning point in the history of the Revolution and the Continent.

With it began the subversion of Europe, which did not end until 1815. Why did it begin with the Italian campaign? Had not the Revolution been at war for five years and already achieved brilliant results? But until then the Revolution had not disturbed the European equilibrium. It had only affected the north and Germany, where its armies found a monarchical system solidly rooted in two dynasties, Austria and Prussia.

The Holy Roman Empire, though no longer holy or an empire or Roman as Voltaire put it, nevertheless had considerable moral force. Germany was also able to resist the revolutionary invasion. In Italy, the situation was quite different, however. The Revolution found there a number of small states, militarily very weak and lacking ties with each other. There was of course an institution that lent spiritual unity to the peninsula: the Papacy. If at the end of the eighteenth century Italy was the only part of Europe in which the civilization of the Middle Ages was still preserved, this was owing to the Papacy.

Everywhere, the Church controlled the political scene. Indeed, the Papacy, a spiritual power, could not impose itself on a temporal power unless the temporal power respected and venerated it. The revolutionary invasion shattered the power of the Church on the peninsula, for the revolutionaries held the Church in contempt. Thus Italy saw itself abandoned by the spiritual forces which had directed it, and the revolutionary spirit was unleashed. However, it was not a question of applying the principles of the Revolution, which, with the exception of a handful of Italians, no one cared about. By revolutionary spirit we must understand the desire and expectation of seizing power outside all principles of legitimacy: seizing it by force and exercising it by terror. Before the Revolution, such an inclination did not exist in Italy, any more than anywhere else. Napoleon and the Directory were themselves frightened of it at first and sought to check it, but in vain. As the French army advanced in the peninsula, the revolutionary groups took the opportunity to destroy the Old Regime and seize the government. It was the formation of these groups that determined the political future of France and obliged it to seize, bit by bit, the entire peninsula. Thus was born the great struggle between France and Austria for the possession of Italy. It was to convulse Europe for many years.

Index

active citizens, definition of, 47
Alexander I of Russia, 69
Ami du Peuple, 57
Antraigues, Count of, 169
aristocracy of regicides, 208–209, 213
assignats, and inflation, 107–108, 112
Augsburg, League of, 121
Aulard, François, 23, 47, 48, 168
Austria, 74, 82, 83, 86, 87, 88, 89, 117, 122, 227; Legislative Assembly's ultimatum to, 84; and French Revolutionary Wars, 89–91, 93, 95–96, 99, 104, 105, 119, 126, 127, 129, 130, 135, 191, 221, 226

Barras, Paul François Jean Nicolas de, 192, 195, 196, 215, 216
Barrère de Vieuzac, Bertrand, 132, 151, 171, 189, 193, 194
Bastille, fall of, 21, 22, 24 27, 28, 33, 51, 64, 115
Belgium, 91, 104, 118, 122, 125, 126, 129, 130, 131, 135, 188, 191, 221
Billaud-Varennes, Jean Nicolas, 194
Bolsheviks, Russian, 23
bourgeoisie, high, 26, 36, 68
bread cards, issue of (1793), 145–146

Brissot, Jacques, 74, 75, 80, 83, 87, 88; quoted, 79
Brunswick, Duke of, 87, 100, 102; manifesto of, 93
Burke, Edmund, 117

Calvinism, 184, 187
Cambon, Joseph, 123, 125, 197; quoted, 123
Campoformio, Treaty of, 69
Carnot, Lazare Nicolas Marguerite, 146, 197
Carrier, Jean Baptiste, 127, 141, 192, 217
Catherine II of Russia, 103
Catholic Church, 41–42, 43, 44, 53–55, 61; *see also* papacy
Chabot, François, 171
Champ-de-Mars riot, 59, 70, 93
Chaumette, Pierre Gaspard, 158, 170
Chauvelin, François, 119
China, 121
Christianity, 7, 54; attacked by French Revolution, 157–158
Civil Constitution of the Clergy, 49, 53, 54, 55, 56, 57, 61
clergy, 33, 35, 36, 39; and Estates-General, 9, 10; isolated from monarchy, 26; opposes Talleyrand's program, 42; *see also* Civil Constitution of
Cloots, Anacharsis, 177

229

INDEX

Coburg, Prince of, 135, 191
commerce, regulatory function of, 159
Committee of Public Safety, 134, 136, 141–146 *passim*, 151, 152, 155, 168, 169, 170, 177, 178, 179, 181, 188, 193; reports on, 168–176, 180, 190–191; Robespierre breaks with, 192; reorganized by Convention, 204
Commune of Paris, 94, 95, 158, 195, 196
communism, 109, 117, 184
Congress of Vienna, 3
conscription, imposed on world by French Revolution, 121
Constituent Assembly, 30–65 *passim*, 68, 91, 98, 108, 143, 175; Estates-General proclaims itself as (1789), 20; and Great Fear, 31, 32, 33, 35, 36; conservative elements eliminated from, 32, 33, 51; passes new laws, 33–34, 37, 41, 45–46; on property as natural right, 34; submits to rioters, 40; weakness of, 40, 61; secularizes wealth of Church, 43–44, 45, 53; contradictions of, 45–46; passes Civil Constitution of the Clergy, 49, 53, 54, 55, 56, 57, 61; mistrust of court and upper classes, 52, 61; panic of, at flight of king, 58; achievements of, 60; succeeded by Legislative Assembly, 60; committees elected by, 62
constitution: voted by Constituent Assembly (1789), 37, 48, 51; voted by Legislative Assembly (1792), 48; voted by Conven-

tion (1793), 142, 145; of year III, 205–209 *passim*, 213, 214, 215, 220; of year VIII, 216, 220
Consulate, 35, 68, 138, 176
Convention, 35, 95–130 *passim*, 131, 133, 136, 138–139, 142, 143, 147, 152, 155, 165, 174, 193, 196, 222; membership of, 98–99; proclaims republic, 100–101; and decree of November 19, 1792, 105; brings charges against king, 110–111; votes death penalty for king, 111–112; on coinage of money, 113–114; re-establishes freedom of navigation in Scheldt, 118; decrees levy for army (1793), 120, 121, 146; Cambon's speech to, 123; adopts proclamation following Cambon's speech, 123–125; creates Revolutionary Tribunal, 129; receives letter from Dumouriez, 129; parliamentary immunity suspended in, 134; price-fixing measures of, 136–137, 160; and uprising of June 2, 1793, 138, 140; threatened by general revolt, 140 decrees *levée en masse* (1793), 146; passes Law of the Maximum, 160, 161, 162; absence of opposition to, 163; passes law of Prairial, 188, 189; Robespierre accused in, 194–195; confronts Commune, 195; outlaws Robespierre, 195; Thermidorian reaction, 203–207, 210, 212, 213; reorganizes Committee of Public Safety, 204; anniversary of king's execution

decreed national holiday, 210; "two-thirds" decrees of, 213, 214, 216; defeats National Guard (1795), 215–216; Sorel's appraisal of, 217–218; seeks unanimity, 218–219, 220; illegitimacy of, as reason for self-contradictions, 219
Corday, Charlotte, 143, 144, 145, 189
Cordeliers, 156, 170, 171, 172, 174
Council of Ancients, 205
Council of Five Hundred, 205
Counter-Reformation, 86
counterrevolution, myth of, 71, 72, 140
Couthon, Georges, 172, 195
Custine, Adam Philippe de, 105, 161

Danton, Georges, 13, 70, 91, 127, 128, 129, 134, 135, 136, 156, 162, 163, 164, 165, 180, 188, 197; quoted, 96; trial and execution of, 181, 183
Dantonists, 163, 164, 167, 171, 172, 220
Declaration of Pilnitz, 71, 75
Declaration of the Rights of Man, 34, 35, 37, 40, 43, 46, 54, 138, 181
De Jure belli et pacis (Grotius), 184
Delessart (Minister of Interior), 77, 81, 84, 87; quoted, 84
Desaix, Louis Charles Antoine, 217
Desmoulins, Camille, 165, 181; quoted, 72–73
Diderot, Denis, 4

Directory, 35, 206, 220, 225, 227
Dumouriez, Charles François, 88, 89, 105, 122, 123, 126, 127, 129, 130, 131, 178

Eglantine, Fabre d', 181
émigrés, 71, 72, 74, 76, 77, 78, 80, 81, 85, 107
Encyclopaedists, 44
England, 121, 188; in struggle with France, 114, 118–119, 126, 172, 173, 178, 188, 191, 221; political evolution in, 115, 116; stability of empirical system in, 116; French Revolution feared in, 117, 118; wealth of, 119
Enragés, 114, 127, 133, 136, 137, 143
Essau philosophique sur le gouvernement civil (Fénelon), 185
Estates-General, 9–15 passim, 19, 20, 21, 24, 26, 51, 58, 63; proclaims itself Constituent Assembly (1789), 20

federalism, 141, 142
Fénelon, François de Salignac de La Mothe, 117, 184, 186; quoted, 185–186
Ferrero, Guglielmo, 65 n.
Festival of Liberty, 158
Feuillants, 69, 80, 81, 149
Fouché, Joseph, 141, 192
Fouquier-Tinville, Antoine Quentin, 180, 188
France: achievements of monarchy in, 25; disorder in, during first French Revolution, 50, 62, 143; and Revolutionary Wars, 89–91, 93, 95–96, 99, 102–

INDEX

France (cont'd.)
106, 114, 118–130, 135–136, 188,
191, 221–223, 224, 225, 226; in
struggle with England, 114,
118–119, 126, 172, 173, 178, 188,
191, 221; doctrine of popular
sovereignty in, 115–116, 117,
143; population of (1792), 119;
revival of monarchical tradition
in, 208, 212; see also French
Revolution
Francis II of Germany, 68–69, 85,
86, 89
Freemasons, 87
freethinkers, 44
French Empire, 35, 176
French Revolution, first, 3–9 passim, 13, 27, 52, 55, 56, 57, 61,
63, 67, 71, 82; version of, by
historians of Left, 4, 5, 6, 27,
31, 38, 47, 89, 110, 112, 123;
version of, by historians of
Right, 4, 5, 6, 27, 31, 48, 65, 89,
112, 123, 125; ambiguous nature
of, 9; causes of, 24–25, 26–27,
63–65; contradictions of, 45–46,
143, 218, 219; and suffrage system, 47; and Europe, 71–88
passim; red flag becomes symbol of, 93; and flight of gold,
113; effects military transformation, 120–121, 225; uses militia,
122; definitive defeat of, 138;
see also France
French Revolution, second, 138,
147, 148, 220; and use of
obscene language, 157; attacks
on Christianity, 157–158; adoption of new calendar, 157–158;
as totalitarian despotism, 181

French Revolutionary Wars, 89–
91, 93, 95–96, 99, 102–106, 114,
118–130, 135–136, 188, 191, 221–
223, 224, 225, 226

Geneva, and Calvinism, 184
Genoa, 168; as republican oligarchy, 101
Germany, 68, 73, 88, 102, 105, 106,
149, 226
Girondists, 69, 71, 72, 74, 79, 80,
85, 86, 87, 88, 110, 111, 127, 133,
136, 137, 139, 145, 156; arrest
of, 138, 140, 155; accused of
federalism, 141; trial and execution of, 161, 162, 177
government: definition of, 24;
legitimate, definition of, 66; see
also revolutionary government
Great Fear, 28–33 passim, 138,
140, 150, 151; Terror as final
convulsion of, 152, 161, 188,
190–191
Grenville, Lord, 118, 168
Grotius, Hugo, 116, 184

Hanriot, François, 138, 180, 195
Hébert, Jacques René, 156, 157,
163, 164, 170, 171, 172, 173,
180, 188, 195; trial and execution of, 174, 177, 178, 179
Hébertists, 157, 158, 159, 162, 163,
164, 165, 167, 171, 172, 220;
trial and execution of, 174, 177,
178, 179
Hénin (French diplomat), 168,
169
Henry VIII of England, 54, 55
Hoche, Louis Lazare, 170, 217

Holland, 118, 126, 221, 222
Holy Roman Empire, 105, 226

inflation, and circulation of assignats, 107–108, 112
international law, 184
Isnard, Maximin, 134
Italy, 126, 149, 225, 226, 227

Jacobins, 69, 72, 77, 80, 91, 107,
133, 145, 146, 148, 156, 174, 204,
208, 210
Jansenists, 44
Japan, 121
Jaurès, Jean Léon, 148; quoted,
149, 179
Joseph II of Belgium, 122
Jourdan, Jean Baptiste, 191, 221,
222

Kaunitz, Prince, 81, 83, 85, 88, 89;
quoted, 81–82, 84, 85
Kléber, Jean Baptiste, 222

Lacroix, Sébastien, 146
Lafayette, Marquis de, 59
Las Casas (Spanish ambassador to
Venice), 168, 169
Legislative Assembly, 60, 66–70
passim, 93, 97, 128, 175; votes
constitution (1792), 48; illegitimacy of, 67, 68; membership
of, 68, 69, 98; intimidated by
extreme Left, 70–71; replies to
Kaunitz, 83–84; and Commune,
94; suspends king, 94
legitimate government, definition
of, 66
Leopold II of Austria, 77, 81, 83,
85, 86, 87, 88

Liége: captured by Austrians, 126,
127; entered by Jourdan, 221
Louis-Philippe, 8
Louis XIII, 25
Louis XIV, 26, 65, 65 n., 122, 222,
224
Louis XVI, 10, 11, 17, 18, 45, 49,
61, 76, 78, 88, 100; declares
Third Estate's decisions uncon-
stitutional, 19; letter to Constituent Assembly (1789), 37;
abduction of, 40; and Civil
Constitution of the Clergy, 56,
57; flight and arrest of, 57–59;
and war with Austria, 89, 91,
92; suspended by Legislative
Assembly, 94; trial and sentencing of, 109–111, 114; and
judgment of posterity, 112;
execution of, 112, 119
Louis XVII, 122; death of, 211–
212
Louis XVIII, 74, 76, 169, 211, 212
Luther, Martin, 55

Maestricht, Holland, 126, 221
Magna Carta, 115
Mandat (head of National
Guard), 93
Marat, Jean Paul, 13, 57, 70, 80,
91, 133, 142, 179; assassination
of, 143, 144, 145
Maratists, 179
Marceau, François Séverin, 217
Marie-Antoinette, 57–58, 79, 81,
110, 157, 161; trial and sentenc-
ing of, 161, 162, 164
Marie-Caroline of Naples, 162
Marseillaise, 92

Mathiez, Albert, 131, 165–166, 168, 169, 183, 200; quoted, 198–199, 201
Middle Ages, 11, 89, 226
Mirabeau, Honoré, 14, 17, 18, 20, 43, 115, 138; quoted, 15–17, 20, 21, 115
Miranda, Francisco, 126, 127
monasticism, 41, 42
Monnier, Luc, 65 n.
Montagnards, 134, 139
Mountain, the, 110, 111, 114, 127, 133, 137, 139, 156, 210, 220
Municipality, 155, 156, 170, 171, 190, 195

Napoleon Bonaparte, 13, 126, 176, 200, 216, 225, 227
Narbonne (Minister of War), 78, 79, 82, 86, 87
National Constituent Assembly, see Constituent Assembly
National Convention, see Convention
National Guard, 49, 59, 92, 93, 107, 138, 156, 195, 196, 208, 212–213, 219; defeated by Convention (1795), 215–216
natural rights, doctrine of, 184–186, 200
Necker, Jacques, 9, 34
Nelson, Horatio, 162
Nicholas II of Russia, 23
nobility, 33, 35, 36, 39, 67; and Estates-General, 9, 10; isolated from monarchy, 26
Not a Moment to Lose (Lacroix), 146

Old Regime, 4, 5, 22, 25, 30, 31, 35, 41, 44, 48, 53, 63, 73, 82, 89, 98, 104, 110, 132, 186, 200, 227; swept away by Constituent Assembly, 60; abolition of controlled economy of, 108, 109; professional armies of, 121; wars waged by, 223–224
Origins of Contemporary France (Taine), 196

papacy, 53, 54, 55, 86, 226; see also Catholic Church
Paris: mob rule in, 36, 37, 44; as center of luxury industries, 39; unemployment crisis in, 39; Commune of, 94, 95, 158, 195, 196; as capital of Revolution, 140; exercises authority, 155–156
passive citizens, definition of, 47
Patriote français, Le, 74
Périer, Casimir, 143, 144
Pétion, Jérôme, 93
Pichégru, Charles, 170
Pitt, William, the Younger, 164, 172, 173, 180
Poland, 103, 104
Prieur-Duvernois, Claude Antoine, 146
property: declared natural right by Constituent Assembly, 34; Robespierre's view of, 186
Protestants, in France, 34, 44
Prussia, 87, 88, 89, 117; and French Revolutionary Wars, 89–91, 93, 95–96, 99, 102–106, 221, 226

Reason, "creed" of, 158
Reflections on the Revolution in France (Burke), 117

Reign of Terror, *see* Terror
religion, attacked by French Revolution, 157–158
Renaud, Cécile, 189
Restoration, 61, 123
revolution: double meaning of, 7; constructive, 8, 9, 17; destructive, 8, 9, 17, 18, 52; and phenomenon of use of obscene language, 157
revolutionary government: definition of, 67; advantages of, in wartime, 120; conditions necessary for, 149–150
Revolutionary Tribunal, 129, 134, 161, 162, 163, 167, 180, 181, 190
Richelieu, Cardinal, 25, 65
Robespierre, Maximilien, 13, 48, 70, 80, 91, 110, 127, 128, 130, 135, 136, 156, 161–162, 163, 164, 167, 168, 170, 171, 172, 177, 180, 181, 183–202; quoted, 77, 187; opposed to Hébertists, 159, 174; and Sieyès, 167–168, 171, 172, 175, 177; judgment concerning, 175, 187, 196–201; and Danton, 180, 183–184; popularity of, 184, 187; on private property, 186; on equality, 186–187; fear for his life, 189; assassination attempts upon, 189; enemies of, 191–192; as deist, 192; break with Committee of Public Safety 192; accused in Convention, 194–195; outlawed by Convention, 195; execution of, 196
Robespierre terroriste (Mathiez), 166

Robespierrists, 159, 163, 164, 172, 198, 201, 220
Roland, Jean Marie, 91
Rousseau, Jean Jacques, 4, 46, 144, 184, 187
Roux, Jacques, 114
Royal Council, 12
Ruhl, 76; quoted, 77
Russia, 68, 88, 117, 175
Russian Revolution, 24, 175

Saint-André, Jean Bon, quoted, 132–133
Saint-Just, Louis Antoine Léon de, 148, 160, 161, 171, 175, 195, 201
sans-culottes, 134
Saxe, Marshal, 122
scholasticism, 184
Sieyès, Abbé, 13, 14, 16, 18, 172, 173, 177, 180; and Napoleon, 13, 176; quoted, 14, 168; and Robespierre, 167–168, 171, 172, 175, 177; judgment concerning, 175–176
Social Contract (Rousseau), 4, 46, 184
socialism, 184, 187
Society for Robespierrist Studies, 183
Sorel, Albert, 63, 64, 65, 89; quoted, 63–64, 65, 217–218
Spain, 169
Spanish Succession, War of, 122
stoicism, 184
suffrage, 47; universal, 95, 142, 143, 145, 207

Taine, Hippolyte, 4, 50, 200; quoted, 148–149, 196–198

Talleyrand, Charles Maurice de, 44, 138; advocates secularization of wealth of Church, 41–46 *passim;* quoted, 60
Tallien, Jean Lambert, 192, 194
tax strike, after fall of Bastille, 42
Tennis Court Oath, 138
Terror, 145, 152, 161, 164, 165, 166, 168, 193, 210; as final convulsion of the Great Fear, 152, 161, 188, 190–191; causes of, 166–167; worst law of, 188; end of, 196, 208
Thermidorean reaction, 204–227 *passim*
Third Estate, 9, 10, 12, 13, 14, 18, 33, 115; proclaims itself National Assembly (1789), 19
Trèves, Elector of, 81, 82
Tuileries, attack on, 92, 93–94

United States of America, 121; republican experiment in, 101; federalism of, 141

universal suffrage, 95, 142, 143, 145, 207

Valmy, Prussian retreat at, 102, 103, 104
Varennes, royal family's flight to, 57–59
Vendée, insurrection in, 131, 132, 166
Venice, 168; as republican oligarchy, 101, 122
Vergniaud, Pierre, 75, 76, 83; quoted, 75
Versailles: opening of Estates-General at (1789), 9, 63; royal family abducted at, 40
Vienna, Congress of, 3
Voltaire, 4, 44, 144, 226

Westphalia, Treaty of, 118
wheat, prices fixed for, 136–137
World War I, 6, 166